TWO BEGINNINGS

2

TWO BEGINNINGS

A BRIEF ACADIAN HISTORY

J. Alphonse Deveau

Lescarbot
Publications

Cover:
The Acadians, Building a home, Belleisle, N. S.
The publisher wishes to thank the Nova Scotia Museum for the cover which depicts the construction of a representative Acadian home of the early 1700s. This is a reproduction of one of a number of watercolours painted by Nova Scotia Museum artist Azor Vienneau in the production of the educational film series, *Premières terres acadiennes*. Other pictures in the series appear on pages 47-54 in this book.
The Nova Scotia Museum has published posters of Mr. Vienneau's work, which can be purchased.

ISBN 0-921443-16-1
Lescarbot Publications
P.O. Box 237
Yarmouth,
Nova Scotia
Canada
B5A 4B2

Editor's note

This work is translated summary of a two part volume entitled "Notre Héritage acadien" published in 1980.

This book was first published in 1980 under the same title "Two Beginnings, A Brief Acadian History."

Photographs and Chapter XIII have been added and minor changes made in other chapters.

The author

Professor J. Alphonse Deveau is the renowned author of 14 major books and numerous articles on Acadian History.

He is the founder and first director of *Le Centre acadien de l'Université Sainte-Anne.* He received an Honorary Doctorate in History from l'Université Sainte-Anne, in Church Point, Nova Scotia.

Now retired after 35 years in teaching he devotes most of his time and energy to historical research and writing.

Contents

Chapter I
Origin of the Name: Acadia or Acadie 9

Chapter II
The Forerunners of Port Royal 13

Chapter III
Port Royal in Acadia - Its Troubled Beginnings 17

Chapter IV
Port Royal, a Victim of Many Conflicts 27

Chapter V
Life at Port Royal 39

Chapter VI
Life at Grand-Pré, Beaubassin and Other Pre-Expulsion Acadian Communities 55

Chapter VII
Religion and Education in Acadia Before 1755 69

Chapter VIII
The Acadian Family 75

Chapter IX
Events Leading to the Expulsion 79

Chapter X
An Examination of the Motives for the Expulsions 97

Chapter XI
The Acadians Maintain Their Ethnic Identity 105

Chapter XII
Acadian Resettlements After the Expulsion 109

Chapter XIII
The Acadians Today 127

Map of Beginnings and Resettlements 137

CHAPTER 1

Origin of the name: Acadia or Acadie

Almost all the names of places and regions in North America are copies of place names in Europe or derivations of Indian words. Acadie or Acadia can be either, or it may be a combination of both.

We first find a word which resembles Acadia in the description of the coast of North America by Janus Verrazano, (as he signed his name), or Jean de Verrazane, a Florentine shipmaster sailing for King Francis I of France. Verrazano sailed from Madeira, Spain, in 1524, with four ships to explore the coast of the new-found continent northwards from the Spanish possessions to the south.

His expedition first landed on the coast of present day Georgia. On his third landing, on the coast of Virginia, he was struck by the beauty of the landscape and named the place Arcadia, that fabled Greek province, famous for its beautiful trees and rolling countryside.

Subsequent map makers, while copying Verrazano's map, (which no longer exists), changed the location and the spelling from the original. For example, Zaltieri's map has Larcadia, in present day Maine.

Finally, according to Ganong, the r would have been dropped to leave the word Acadia.

Other authors trace the origin of the word Acadia, or Acadie, to either the Malecite word "quoddy" meaning a fertile place, or the Micmac "algatig", a camp site. In fact there are a number of places in the Acadian peninsula ending in "acadie" or "quoddy", such as Shubenacadie, Tracadie, Nacadie, and Passamaquoddy, which is often found as Pesmacadie on old maps.

It would have been possible for French fishermen and fur traders who had been coming to these shores for many years before Verrazano to have heard the Indians using their words for "camp site" and "fertile place", and to have thought that this word designated the territory.

These Frenchmen would in turn give their own pronunciation to the Indian words they heard, and would have reported back to their superiors in France about the abundance of furs and fish in "La Cadie".

Be that as it may, the monopoly of the fur trade granted by letters patent to Sieur de Monts by Henry IV of France, in 1603, clearly speaks of "La Cadie". Champlain first uses "Accadie" then "Acadie".

Whatever the origin of the word, it is widely used today throughout the Maritimes, in Québec, in Louisiana and in France. There is an Acadian car, an Acadia University, Acadian Lines, Editions d'Acadie, Acadia Colliery, Village Acadien, Acadian Parish in Louisiana and paroisse Acadie, near Montreal, the ferry boat "Acadie" in France. In spite of its obscure origin the name has found a wide and varied acceptance on two continents.

Such a widespread use is in part due to the history of the people and the territory it designated, which will be the subject of the following chapters.

SOURCES OF INFORMATION

Samuel de Champlain - *Les Voyages de Champlain dans Oeuvres de Champlain* - Québec, 1870 - réimprimé Éditions du Jour, Montréal 1973.

C. Payette - *Old French Papers* - Montreal 1966.

John Quinpool - *First Things in Acadia* -Halifax 1936.

Public Archives of Canada, Ottawa.

CHAPTER II

The Forerunners of Port Royal

Even before Verrazano's voyage, another Frenchman, the Baron de Lery, had set sail in 1518 to establish a colony in the New World which would serve as a refuge for French Protestants during the period of religious persecutions in France.

He landed at Canso, then pushed on to seek a better place, but instead landed at Sable Island, where he supposedly left some animals, and then returned to France.

The next French explorer, Jacques Cartier, sailed from St. Malo, in 1534, as an agent of the Admiral of France, Philippe de Brion-Chabot. On this voyage Cartier sighted Newfoundland, the coast of Labrador, Prince Edward Island and landed at Gaspé, where he planted a large cross, claiming the country for France. Cartier made another voyage in 1535. This time he went up the Saint Lawrence as far as as the Indian village of Hochelaga, at the foot of Mount Royal, the site of present day Montreal. The expedition then returned to the Indian village of Stadacona, (Québec) and decided to winter there. For the first time Europeans got a real taste of a Canadian winter, one for which they were not prepared. By mid-November the river was frozen solid and snow was piling on the decks. It was not long before almost all the men were down with scurvy. Twenty-five of them died before the Indians showed Cartier how to cure the disease with a simple remedy made by steeping the bark and needles of white cedar. When the ice broke Cartier returned to France to report to his king.

In spite of the dismal report Cartier must have given, the king was determined to try again to set up a colony in the New World. Consequently he commissioned Jean-Francois de la Rocque, Sieur de Roberval, to head an expedition to the Saint Lawrence. Roberval chose Jacques Cartier as his chief captain, and convicts and paupers from the streets of Paris and other cities as his colonists. Cartier sailed first to prepare for the coming of Roberval and his colonists. However the latter delayed a year, and when he reached St. John's, Newfoundland, found Cartier there ready to return to France. Roberval ordered Cartier to turn back with him, but the latter would have none of it and slipped away from his commander at night. Roberval continued on his way and set up his colony at Tadoussac, where fishermen and fur traders had left a few shacks. Roberval proved to be a harsh and cruel man, and caused great hardships among the ill-prepared colony, which included women and children. In 1543, the remnant of the colony was rescued by an expedition again headed by Jacques Cartier.

The next three colonizing attempts by Frenchmen had one aim; to establish a refuge for French Protestants.

In 1562, Jean Ribaut sailed with a group of French Huguenots and established the first Port Royal in America, not in Nova Scotia, but on the coast of Northern Florida. It seems that the would-be colonists has second thoughts as soon as they arrived and decided to return to France, only to be captured by an English ship and brought to England, whence they eventually made their way home.

Two years later, René de Laudonière, who was with Ribaut in the previous expedition established Fort Caroline, further north than Ribault's Port Royal. With him were a large number of French Huguenots. This colony was short-lived, for it fell to a combined attack by the Spaniards and Indians, and a large number of Frenchmen were killed. Laudonière left a vivid description of this attack. It is found in *Old French Papers* by B.C. Payette.

A third attempt at a similar religious colony was made in 1598 by the Marquis de la Roche, a Protestant gentlemen. To find the required manual labourers for such a colony, the Marquis recruited some 50 convicts from the seaport prisons of

France. These he left on Sable Island with one officer, named Querbonoyer, and set out to find a better location. However, storms drove his ship back to France where he was promptly jailed. (During this troubled time in France, de la Roche happened to be on the losing side of politics). Meanwhile the fifty former convicts on Sable Island fared miserably. Five years passed before a ship was sent from France to repatriate the eleven survivors of the fifty left there.

Had these attempted colonies by the Huguenots succeeded, the eastern seaboard of North America might today be a French Protestant stronghold. However these would-be colonizers lacked the most basic requirements for a successful colony: skilled tradesmen, men who knew the country, tillers of the soil, families, and strong financial backing in the homeland.

By the 1600's the need for such colonies had disappeared. France had some degree of religious tolerance with the crowning of Henry IV, the former Protestant leader, as King of France, and now the Huguenots had a measure of security in designated cities in their native land. However, the fur trade offered a new attraction to venturesome Frenchmen, and this interest eventually brought about the founding of a second French Port Royal in America.

SOURCES OF INFORMATION

Père C. Cormier - *L'Origine et l'histoire du nom Acadie, avec un discours sur les autres noms de lieux acadiens* - Moncton 1966.

Henri Froidevaux - *Origine du mot Acadie* - 1920

W. F. Ganong - *The Origin of the Place Names Acadia and Norembega*

B.C. Payette - *Old French Papers* - Montreal, 1966.

John Quinpool - *First Things in Acadia* - Halifax, N.S. 1936.

E.H. Wilkins - *Arcadia in America* (1957).

CHAPTER III

Port Royal in Acadia
Its Troubled Beginnings

The fishermen from the Basque country, from Brittany and Normandy, who came ashore in Acadia during the summer months to dry their fish, found that they could carry on a profitable trade with the Indians, exchanging knives, axes, pots and cloth for furs. A beaver robe, that could be bartered for an axe or a knife worth a few dollars, could be sold in Paris for the equivalent of $200.00.

With such profits possible, many fishermen and their backers turned to the fur trade, which was not only far more profitable but also easier to carry out. However, such a lucrative trade also attracted the attention of some gentlemen of the court who had influence with the king. The king had the power to grant monopolies, the sole right to trade in certain commodities. These monopolies were granted in return for favours rendered to the crown.

Aymar de Chastes, commander of the Order of St. John had been an ardent supporter of Henry IV during his battles to gain the throne of France and it was to him that the king first gave a patent to settle a colony in the New World in return for the monopoly of the fur trade. De Chastes formed a corporation for the purpose of exploiting the fur trade. He recruited Samuel de Champlain, a geographer, to make a survey of the New World and determine the best place for a fur trading colony. Among the members of the corporation was a shrewd sea captain, François Gravé, Sieur du Pont, who with Pierre Chauvin had established a short-lived colony at Tadoussac in 1600.

It was therefore to this area that François du Pont, or as he most often was called, Pontgravé, directed the de Chastes expedition in 1603, where it arrived on May 24. The expedition continued up the Saint Lawrence to Québec, making friendly contacts with the Indians along the way; then turned back to Tadoussac and sailed for France where it arrived on August 16, 1603, only to learn that their backer, Aymar de Chastes, had passed away a few weeks earlier.

This could have meant a long interruption in the French settlement of the New World had not Champlain become so enthused with the country. He prevailed upon Henry IV to find another nobleman to undertake a settlement in America.

The king's choice fell upon another of his early supporters, Pierre du Gua, Sieur de Monts, governor of the city of Pons. De Monts, a Huguenot, had also been with Chauvin at Tadoussac. He was a nobleman of some means, having married a wealthy young woman.

He was also practical and shrewd, and apart from his own personal fortune he acquired financial backing by forming a joint stock company among the merchants of Rouen, St. Malo, La Rochelle, and Saint Jean de Luz. Moreover, he was able to profit from the errors of judgment and from the sad experiences of the earlier explorers. The failures of Roberval and Chauvin at Tadoussac showed that it was not wise to attempt a colony in those northern latitudes. The disastrous results that befell Ribaut and Laudonière in the southern latitudes proved that the French had to stay far enough north of the well-established Spanish colonies. Sable Island was now a well-known disaster area. The most promising territory would be the mainland between New Spain to the south and Tadoussac to the north, an area known as La Cadie. So it was to La Cadie that De Monts was granted a monopoly of the fur trade, along with the title of lieutenant-general of the territory from the 40th parallel to the 46th, in return for colonizing and exploring the said territory and converting the native people to Christianity.

De Monts carefully prepared his expedition to the New World. He first had notices posted in all the ports of France forbidding trade in the territory in which he had a monopoly, He then recruited 120 skilled workers (artisans) and chartered two ships, one under the command of Pontgravé, while he was in charge of the other. With him were Champlain, Poutrincourt, Boulai, and the master of the vessel, Champdoré. He brought along two Catholic priests and a Protestant minster.

The two ships sailed from Le Havre in March, 1604 and arrived at Sable Island on May 1st. Pontgravé's ship went to Canso, while De Monts and Champlain explored the coast of Nova Scotia. Champlain mapped and described in detail the sawtooth coast of the peninsula from La Hève to Saint Mary's Bay. Many places along the coast still retain the names given by Champlain.

The expedition left Saint Mary's Bay by the "Petit Passage" and entered the Bay of Fundy, then penetrated into the Annapolis Basin. Poutrincout was especially struck by the advantages that the area offered for a settlement, and asked De Monts if he could have this area for a colony of his own, and De Monts agreed.

The expedition kept on its way all along the shores of the Bay of Fundy, arriving at the mouth of the Saint John River on June 24th. Further along the coast, an island at the mouth of a fairly large river attracted the attention of the commander, and he named the river and the island Sainte-Croix.

True to the conditions of his charter, De Monts continued his voyage of exploration as far as Cape Cod. Having found no location which seemed to offer more advantages than Sainte-Croix Island,the expedition returned there and set about clearing the land and erecting buildings. Meanwhile Pontgravé and Poutrincout had returned to France with one of the ships, laden with furs and some forty of the 120 men of the expedition.

An early winter soon proved the error of De Monts' choice. The buildings were exposed to the chilly northwinds, drifting ice prevented access to the mainland, and the island offered no game to supplement the steady diet of salt meat. Scurvy soon made its appearance and thirty-six of the seventy-nine men died from it before spring arrived.

De Monts had had enough of Sainte-Croix, and as soon as Pontgravé arrived from France with supplies and 40 more men, the whole company crossed over to the site selected the year before by Poutrincourt, bringing with them a good part of the buildings of Sainte-Croix. It was the first transportation of prefabricated buildings in eastern Canada.

The site chosen for the new establishment was opposite Goat Island in the Annapolis Basin, at a place now known as Port Royal.

As already mentioned, Poutrincourt had noticed the advantages of the region and had asked De Monts to grant him the area, to which request the commander agreed.

The artisans reassembled the buildings brought from Sainte-Croix in the form of a hollow square, with a gun platform jutting out from one corner, and a palisade to guard the door on the other.

Once the buildings were finished De Monts and Poutrincourt returned to France, leaving Pontgravé and Champlain in charge of the colony during his absence.

Pontgravé, ever the shrewd trader, began bargaining with the Micmac Indians for the skins of moose, beaver and others.

They fared much better at Port Royal than at Sainte-Croix. As can be readily seen from the plan of the Habitation, they had a good supply of water right in the court yard, and an abundant supply of fuel at their back door. Game was readily available and the friendly Indians were frequent visitors who brought them fresh meat, in exchange for French bread to which, they, the Indians, had taken a liking. However the Frenchmen had not yet completely overcome the dangers of wintering in Acadia, as Champlain reports that six of the men fell victim to scurvy.

In the spring of 1606, Pontgravé had his craftsmen (artisans) build a boat to set out on another voyage of exploration while waiting for De Monts to arrive with supplies. It was the first vessel built in Canada. However storms and rough seas drove them back, and they abandoned the venture. Meanwhile the colonists were anxiously awaiting supplies from France, as spring was already past and there was no sign of De Monts' ships.

Poutrincourt finally arrived in early summer, with fresh supplies and seeds to plant in the virgin soil of the shores of the Rivière Dauphin, the present Annapolis Basin and River. These were the first crops planted on Canadian soil, as far as can be authenticated.

Poutrincourt also brought with him Marc Lescarbot, lawyer and writer and a born leader, Daniel Hay, a surgeon, Louis Hebert, apothecary from Paris, and possibly Claude de La Tour and his son Charles, who was to play a large role in the early history of Acadia.

As one of De Monts' mandates in his commission was to fully explore the territory over which he exercised a monopoly, and which the King of France claimed, the commander of the colony had instructed Poutrincourt to lead an expedition along the coast of Norembega (present day New England) to find an alternate place to settle. It must be remembered that Port Royal was to be Poutrincourt's domain.

Consequently, as soon as the crops were in the ground, Poutrincourt and Champlain left with the ship and most of the men, on another voyage of exploration. This one almost ended in complete disaster as on October 15, at a place which Champlain calls Port Fortuné (at 40 degrees of latitude) and which some historians identify as the port of Chatham on the American seaboard, the expedition was attacked by the Indians and suffered a number of casualties. Champlain has left a vivid description of the battle which ensued, and speaks of the loss of a number of his men.

During their absence Lescarbot kept the other colonists busy tending the garden, improving the buildings, digging a drainage ditch around the Habitation, and opening paths through the woods.

Lescarbot also kept busy in other ways, and had written and directed a play with which to greet Poutrincourt and Champlain and the rest of the explorers on their return.

The sight of a troupe of actors, dressed as Neptune and the Tritons, sailing out to greet the explorers must have lifted the spirits of Champlain and Poutrincourt, who were returning after a rather disastrous expedition.

Neptune, played by Lescarbot himself began by these words:

Arrête Sagamos, arrête toy ici
Et regardes un Dieu qui a de toy souci
Si tu ne me connais, Saturne fut mon père
Je suis de Jupiter et de Pluton le frère

Stop, Sagamos (friend) stop here
And look at the god which cared for you.
If you do not know me, Saturn was my father
I am the brother of Jupiter and Pluto.

The play continues exalting the merits of Poutrincourt and Champlain and their companions for a long time. While it has little literary merit, this play "Le Theâtre de Neptune" remains the first recorded theatre performance on Canadian soil.

Poutrincourt and Champlain were also delighted to notice the armories of France hanging over the doorway of the Habitation.

After the crops were gathered the colonists were well prepared for the winter, which seems to have been unusually mild. To keep up the spirit of the little group, and also to assure a supply of fresh meat, Champlain and Lescarbot organized "l'Ordre du Bon Temps", "The Order of Good Cheer", the first social club in America, north of the Gulf of Mexico, as far as can be ascertained.

According to the rules of the Order, each day one of the group was in charge of providing the food for the whole company of gentlemen (but not the artisans), and it was his duty to get out and hunt to have fresh game for the table. The Indian chief, Membertou, was a frequent guest at the gentlemen's table.

When spring arrived the men, with high hopes, set about enlarging the garden, Poutrincourt had a mill built on the Lequille River. The inscription on the monument to commemorate the event reads:

To relieve the toil of the hand-mill in making flour for the settlers at Port-Royal, Sieur de Poutrincourt had a water-mill erected on the Lequille River near here early in 1607.

Everything was looking well for the colony. The number of casualties due to scurvy had been reduced to four during the past winter. The land was fertile beyond expectations, and relations with the Indians in Acadia were most friendly. New settlers were expected to arrive with De Monts' ship.

But alas! De Monts' ship brought orders to abandon the colony and return bag and baggage to France. De Monts' enemies in France had succeeded in having his monopoly revoked, so that the colony was no longer feasible.

It was therefore "with great grief in their hearts," as Lescarbot says, that the colonists left Port Royal on August, 11th, 1607, and thus ended the first chapter in the tumultuous history of France's second Port Royal in North America.

SOURCES OF INFORMATION

Antonio Dragon - *L'Acadie et ses 40 Robes noires* - Bellarmin, Montréal, 1973

L'Abbé Azarie Couillard-Després - *En marge de la tragédie d'un peuple, d'Emile Lauvrière, Observation sur l'Histoire de l'Acadie Françoise de M. Moreau, Paris 1873, Montréal 1919. Charles de Saint-Etienne de La Tour au tribunal de l'histoire. Charles de St. Etienne de La Tour et son temps 1593-1666.*

Père Clarence J. d'Entremont - *Petit Manuel d'Histoire d'Acadie des débuts à 1670*, Université de Moncton, 1977, Moncton, N.B.

Nicolas Denys - *Description des Costes de l'Amérique Septentrionale.*

Public Archives of N.S. - *Minutes of His Majesty's Council at Annapolis Royal 1736-1749.*

Public Archives of Canada.

Emile Lauvrière - *La Tragédie d'un peuple - Histoire du peuple acadien de ses origines à nos jours*, Editions Bossard, Paris, 1932.

Antoine Bernard - *Le Drame acadien depuis 1604*, Les Clercs de Saint-Viateur, Montréal, 1936.

Rameau de Saint-Père - *Une colonie féodale en Amérique. La France aux Colonies*, A Jouby, Librairie Editeur, Paris, 1859.

Beamish Murdoch - *A History of Nova Scotia or Acadie*, Vol. 1 James Barnes, printer, Halifax, N.S. 1865.

Marc Lescarbot - *Histoire de la Nouvelle-France*, Paris, 1617. Livre IV. Translation by P. Erondelle in *Nova Francia*.

Andrew Hill Clark - *Acadia, The Geography of Early Nova Scotia to 1760*, The University of Winsconsin Press, Madison, Wis. 1968.

Lucien Campeau, S.J. - *La première mission d'Acadie 1602-1616*, Les Presses de l'Université Laval, Cité Universitaire, Québec, 10e, 1967.

CHAPTER IV

Port Royal, a Victim of Many Conflicts

When one looks at the peaceful pastoral country of the Annapolis Basin, one cannot imagine that these shores changed hands more times, and were the scene of more military actions, than possibly any other place in North America.

We have seen that De Monts had to abandon his venture at Port Royal in 1607, due to the loss of his monopoly, because of the pressure his enemies in France exerted on the king.

In 1610 the venture was revived by Jean de Biencourt, Sieur de Poutrincourt, primarily for the establishment of a fur trading post, but with a very definite commitment of converting the Indians and of bringing in settlers.

With Poutrincourt came his son, Charles de Biencourt, (henceforth referred to as Biencourt) Claude de La Tour and his son Charles and l'abbé Jessé Fléché. Later came Louis Hébert, the apothecary of Paris, destined to become the first farmer in Acadia and then, sometime later, in Quebec.

The new colony had the blessing of the King of France and the monopoly of the fur trade, but no firm financial backing from the court. De Monts had helped out by relinquishing all his claims to the Port Royal area. On the other hand, Poutrincourt found financial backers, two Huguenot merchants, Duquesne and Desjardins, who would share in the profits of the monopoly, on condition that Poutrincourt would have to bring two Jesuit missionaries to convert the natives to Christianity, which in this case would mean the Catholic Faith. The Huguenot merchants threatened to withdraw their support if the Jesuits were a party to the expedition; however, they accepted l'Abbé Fléché, a secular priest.

The good Abbé succeeded beyond all expectations in the field of conversions. Soon after his arrival he baptized Chief Membertou and twenty members of his family. Soon many other Indian families sought baptism, so that from his arrival in the colony in the summer of 1610 to his departure in 1611, l'Abbé Fléché had baptized more than 130 Indians.

In the summer of 1611, Charles de Biencourt returned to France bringing a shipload of furs and a good report concerning the work of christianizing the native people. This report greatly impressed Antoinette du Pons, Madame de Guercheville, a lady-in-waiting to the Queen and a very devout person. On the advice of her spiritual counsellor, the Jesuit, Father Coton, she bought out the shares of the Huguenot merchants and gave them to the Jesuits, and also furnished the necessary capital to maintain the colony of Port Royal for another year.

Two Jesuit priests, Biard and Massé, sailed with Biencourt and Louis Hébert for Port Royal on the "Grâce de Dieu" arriving during the summer of 1611. L'Abbé Fléché returned to France with Poutrincourt.

At first the Jesuits were full of admiration for the courage and know-how of young Biencourt. Soon, however, relations between the two deteriorated and sowed the seeds of future conflicts.

The Jesuits were scandalized by the lack of religious instructions received by the baptized Indians, and then rebuffed by Biencourt, who did not intend to share the material administration of the colony with them, even though they had shares in the venture. Biencourt accused the Jesuits of connivance with French adventurers who were trading illegally with the Indians at the mouth of the Saint John River. Relations continued to worsen until the Jesuits "went on strike" and refused to administer the sacraments. Biencourt went further and imprisoned them. However, on the 24th of June, 1612, a reconciliation took place, but not before Frère du Thet, a Jesuit Brother who had arrived that summer, had prepared a report on the state of affairs in the colony.

Frère du Thet returned to France on the same ship that had brought him to Port Royal. When his report reached Madame Guercheville, she decided to withdraw her support from Poutrincourt's colony and establish her own further south at the mouth of the Penobscot River, Mount Desert Island. She would name this colony Saint-Sauveur.

Meanwhile Poutrincourt was trying to get other backers for Port Royal, but without success, and so was unable to send a supply ship in the Fall of 1612. The colonists spent a miserable winter on the Habitation, subsisting on their own meager resources and some help from the Indians.

In the spring the eager watchers saw a ship coming up the basin. They rejoiced when they could see the name "Fleur de Mai". But their rejoicing was short-lived, for this was the ship sent by Madame de Guercheville with colonists and supplies to establish Saint Sauveur. Instead of leaving supplies it took on board Fathers Biard and Massé, the supplies belonging to the Jesuits, and the ornaments of the chapel. The "Fleur de Mai", under the command of Captain Le Coq, Sieur de la Sausaye, sailed on to the site of Saint Sauveur. There the expedition, under the direction of Frère du Thet, immediately quarrelled about what work to undertake first. Some wanted to take advantage of the season and make a clearing to plant a crop, while others wanted to build a fort.

This indecision ended abruptly when Captain Samuel Argall and his crew fell upon the unsuspecting and unprepared would-be colonists, and sacked whatever buildings had been put up, and set the "Fleur de Mai" ablaze. Frère du Thet was killed trying to defend the ship. Half the settlers with Father Massé were sent adrift in a small boat and the other half with Father Biard were taken as prisoners to Jamestown, Virginia. Governor Thomas Dale of Virginia approved the raid by Argall, on the pretext that the colony was an intrusion on the territory of Virginia, and kept the prisoners. Later the same year he sent Argall up the coast again, to destroy any French settlement he could find. This time Argall reached Sainte-Croix where he destroyed the remnants of De Monts' Habitation and crossed over to Port Royal, where he found the habitation unguarded. There he took all he could, destroyed the crops, and burned the buildings. Bi-

Lequille, arrived on the scene of destruction just as Argall was sailing away. It seems they got a close enough look at the ship to recognize Father Biard on deck, for Biencourt later accused the Jesuit of having informed Argall about Port Royal. The Jesuits in their Relations defended Biard, saying it was an Indian captured at Sainte-Croix who had informed the raider.

This was the first of many violent actions on the shores of the Basin. Although it destroyed the Habitation, it did not wipe out the colony, for Biencourt and his men remained in the area of Port Royal. The mill at Lequille was still intact, and Poutrincourt found the settlers living in miserable hovels in the area of present day Annapolis, when he made his last voyage to the colony in 1614.

After that, a thick curtain descends on the activities of these early French pioneers of Port Royal, but we know from the reports of the missionaries that they remained in the area, and kept a continuous French presence in Acadia in spite of the total neglect of the mother country.

The Kingdom of France had other more pressing preoccupations at home. King Henry IV had been assassinated in 1610, to be succeeded by his nine year old son. It was a period of unrest within the kingdom, beset with uprising by the Protestants within, and engaged in the Thirty Years War on its eastern frontier.

The conditions were, therefore, ripe for the other claimant to the North American continent, the King of Great Britain, James I, to push his claim. Consequently, in 1621 by Royal Charter, Acadia became the British possession of Nova Scotia and was granted to Sir William Alexander.

However, Sir William Alexander was not able to send out colonists to his Nova Scotia before 1628. The 70 colonists from Scotland, led by William Alexander Jr. quite naturally chose the site already cleared by the French, at what is now Port Royal. There they built a small fort, which they called Charles Fort on an elevation about 500 yards above the ruins of Champlain's Habitation, and set about cultivating the land.

The venture was ill-timed, for on April 29, 1629, the Treaty of Suze was signed bringing peace between England and France, and in March, 1632, the Treaty of St. Germain en Laye restored Acadia to France. Sir William Alexander was instructed, even in 1631, by the King of England to demolish the fort and to remove all the people, goods, cattle and ammunitions from the place, and leave it as deserted as when his son arrived there to settle the place.

It does appear that these colonists were reluctant to leave the place, for a detachment from Charles Fort led by Andrew Forester crossed over to the St. John River and captured a fort that the La Tours had set up there.

In the spring of 1632, Isaac de Razilly, with his lieutenants, Charles de Menou, Sieur d'Aulnay and Charnisay, and Nicolas Denys brought some 300 "hommes d'élites", (no doubt skilled craftsmen) to build a colony at La Have.

One of his first duties was to take possession of the whole territory under his command, as far as the Kennebec River in present day Maine. He also saw to the removal of the Scot settlers who were repatriated to their native Scotland, very probably by d'Aulnay, as he appears to have returned to Europe in 1632, according to the Gazette of Renaudat.

After the death of Razilly in 1635, Charles de Menou , or as he is often known, d'Aulnay, assumed control of the colony. To keep peace among the three rival pretenders to the control of the Acadian territory, the government of France divided Acadia into three areas of control. D'Aulnay, who had succeeded Razilly, would retain the La Have area and the Port Royal region and would have control of the area north of the Baie Française, (present day southern New Brunswick) except a strip along the Saint John River which was granted to Charles de La Tour. The latter would retain a portion of the mainland of Nova Scotia and the Saint John River valley. Nicolas Denys would have control of the eastern portion of Acadia from Canso to Cap des Rosiers in Gaspé.

These enclaves in each other's territory was a built-in cause of dispute between two head-strong and energetic leaders, as were La Tour and d'Aulnay, and it was not long before the misunderstandings broke out in armed conflict, with Port Royal as the main theatre of action.

It must be pointed out here that sometime between 1636 and 1640, d'Aulnay removed most of the settlers of La Have to the Annapolis Basin area, not to the site of Champlain's Habitation, but on a point of land where the Lequille River meets the Annapolis, or to use the names of the period, where the Rivière Allain flowed into the Rivière Dauphin.

The conflict between d'Aulnay and La Tour erupted in 1639, when La Tour captured a ship sent by d'Aulnay to relieve his post of Pentagoët (Penobscot) under attack by the New Englanders. (La Tour pretended that Pentagoët was rightly his).

The conflict shifted to Port Royal the following year, when La Tour attacked the fort with two armed ships that he had hired from Boston merchants. However it was he who was captured by the governor, d'Aulnay, who had just returned from Pentagoët with two armed vessels. La Tour and his men were imprisoned at Port Royal for a time, then released.

In 1642 d'Aulnay destroyed all of La Tour's buildings at Fort St. Louis (now Villagedale, Shelburne County). In reprisal La Tour attacked Port Royal again in the following year with the help of four armed ships from Plymouth, Mass. and one from La Rochelle, France. The fort resisted the attack, but seven of the defenders were wounded, three were killed, and La Tour and his allies broke into the warehouses and took all the furs that were stored to a value of 18,000 pounds. According to the Capuchin Fathers who left a description of the affair, the spoils were divided between La Tour and the New Englanders, the latter got two thirds of the furs.

The denouement of the struggle took place at La Tour's fort at Jemseg on the Saint John River, when, during La Tour's absence, d'Aulnay attacked the place with a superior force and captured the fort which was defended by Madame La Tour. He then proceeded to hang the garrison, sparing only one of its men who acted as hangman of the others. Madame La Tour died not long after the disaster and La Tour left Acadia as a ruined man.

D'Aulnay did not enjoy sole control of the western two thirds of Acadia very long, for he died in 1650 from exposure after a canoe upset on the shores of the Rivière Dauphin.

Soon after d'Aulnay's death Emmanuel Le Borgne, d'Aulnay's principal creditor in France came to Port Royal, and on the pretext of collecting his debts, to the value of 205,286 pounds, he stripped Port Royal of all d'Aulnay's assets, leaving Madame d'Aulnay and her children destitute.

Meanwhile Charles de La Tour had gone to France and had successfully defended himself against all the accusations of d'Aulnay and his supporters. He then returned to Port Royal, with the commission of lieutenant-governor of Acadia. There were now three claimants to Port Royal, Madame d'Aulnay, Emmanuel le Borgne, and Charles de La Tour.

In 1653 Charles de La Tour solved part of the problem by marrying Madame d'Aulnay, thereby settling once and for all, the rival claims of these two families. He and his bride left Port Royal for La Tour's fort at Jemseg, and d'Aulnay's children returned to France.

The following year Emmanuel Le Borgne again entered the picture. This time he took possession of Port Royal, La Have, Pentagoët and even all of the holdings of Nicolas Denys. However he did not hold these long, for the same year a British fleet commanded by Robert Sedgewick suddenly appeared before Port Royal, which was in no condition to defend itself. Le Borgne was taken prisoner and Port Royal again came under British domination. The Acadian settlers remained and were left to administer themselves by a council presided over by Guillaume Trahan.

From 1654 to 1667, the British remained in possession of Port Royal and all of Acadia. Charles de La Tour, with Sir

Thomas Temple and William Crowne, shared control of the territory. (Charles de La Tour, at this time, used the titles conferred upon him by the British sovereign in 1630 to his advantage).

In 1670, a French force under Marson, lieutenant to Hubert d'Andigny, lieutenant-governor of Acadia, reoccupied Port Royal, which thereby changed hands for a fifth time.

In 1690, the cannons of Port Royal growled anew, this time without being able to prevent Sir William Phipps from capturing the fort, burning and looting the settlement. Menneval, the French governor, and his men were taken to Boston.

The following year, 1691, Villebon, coming from Quebec with a small force, captured Port Royal and Edward Tyng, the English governor, was taken prisoner. The Treaty of Ryswick in 1697 officially returned Acadia to France.

The fort had to defend itself again in 1704 against the troops of Colonel Church, who had to retreat after having pillaged and burned many houses and taken about thirty prisoners among the Acadian settlers.

In June 1707, Colonel Marsh, with a strong army and a powerful fleet besieged Port Royal. The defenders, commanded by Daniel Auger, Sieur de Subercase, and supported by St. Castin and 150 Abenaquis, repulsed the attacks against the bastions of the fort. After having suffered heavy losses, Colonel Marsh retreated from Port Royal to Casco, Maine.

Cannon balls struck again against the walls of the fort in August 1707, when a combined force from England and New England, including the forces of Colonel March, entered Annapolis Basin, This combined force, totaling 2000 men and 20 ships was commanded by Col. Wainwright. Subercase had been warned by a French privateer of the coming attack and was ready to receive them.

Here are eyewitness accounts of this siege, reported by Dièreville:

On the 25th of August, the bombs discharged from the fort compelled the English to quit their encampment and they then took up positions opposite the fort. Subercase gave them no rest in this position, as he saw their endeavours to erect their batteries of cannon and mortar. On the 26th they removed half a league lower down. Then the governor sent out a detachment which killed three of their sentries and obliged them to decamp a third time.

At sunrise the English went ashore on the fort side, under the protection of the guns of their fleet and at once began their march. Before them was a point of land covered with woods, in which the Baron de St. Castin lay in ambush with 150 men. He suffered them to approach within pistol shot and then fired three consecutive volleys. They bore the fire with an intrepidity, which he had not expected and appeared resolved to force a passage at whatever loss, but eventually they desisted and a little while after they were seen on the retreat.

Meanwhile, some of the English officers, ashamed at the retreat of their men before inferior numbers, rallied them and brought them back on the French, who then retreated towards the woods because St. Castin and another French officer had both been wounded. The French, seeing the enemy coming back, faced round and showed so much resolution that the English dared not come at close quarters but fired several volleys and withdrew again.

At the end of an hour, Subercase sent a fellow named Granger, an inhabitant and a very brave man, to head Boularderie's detachment and attack the English, who did not wait for his coming but embarked in confusion.

The same day the greater part of the fleet hoisted their anchors and went out of the basin, and on the first of September the whole English fleet was outside. The siege had lasted fifteen days. The French acknowledged three men killed and wounded, the English sixteen killed and as many wounded.

In 1710, Colonel Nicholson directed a strong attack against Port Royal, which, this time, was unable to offer a sustained defence. It had not received any supplies nor payment for its troops since 1707. It was a sombre ending for Subercase who had defended it brilliantly on three other occasions.

After the capture of the fort, Colonel Samuel Vetch remained at Port Royal as governor with 450 soldiers.

Port Royal became Fort Anne in honour of Queen Anne of England.

The following year, 1711, Baron de St. Castin, coming from Pentagoët, with a band of Abenakis, launched an attack against the fort and surprised and defeated a detachment of 80 British soldiers at Bloody Ridge near Bridgetown. However he did not receive the cannons which he had been promised by the governor of Quebec. It being useless to attack the fort without cannons, he gave up the siege of Fort Anne, which had but a small detachment of soldiers at the time.

In 1713 Port Royal was definitely ceded to England by the Treaty of Utrecht.

In 1744, Duvivier arrived from Quebec with 900 soldiers and militiamen but without cannons and attacked the fort. A French fleet coming from Louisbourg was to bring the required cannons but it arrived too late. An English fleet was already in the basin and Duvivier had left with his troops.

In 1745, a last attack was directed against Fort Anne by Capt. Paul Marin from Quebec at the head of 200 militiamen and 40 Indians. Not receiving the cannons which he had been promised, his attempt had no chance of success and he retreated without striking a blow.

While most of the inhabitants of the Port Royal area, settled along the banks of the river, did not take an active part in the military actions, the progress of the colony was delayed a great deal, both during the French Regime and following the British occupation. The last attempts by the French forces to recapture Port Royal increased the desire of the authorities to rid the province of the Acadian population, which they regarded as a potential threat should they abandon their policy of neutrality.

SOURCES OF INFORMATION

Dièreville - *Voyage en Acadie* - Edited by L. U. Fontaine, Québec 1885, pp. 43-67.

Jean-Claude Dupont - "Les défricheurs d'eau" in *Culture vivante*, XXVII, décembre 1972.

Père Clarence J. d'Entremont - *Petit Manuel d'Histoire d'Acadie des débuts à 1670*, Université de Moncton, 1977, Moncton, N.-B.

Nicolas Denys - *Description des Costes de l'Amérique Septentrionale.*

Public Archives of N.S. - Minutes of His Majesty's Council at Annapolis Royal 1736-1749.

Andrew Hill Clark - *Acadia, The Geography of Early Nova Scotia to 1760*, The University of Wisconsin Press, Madison, Wis. 1968.

Lucien Campeau, S.J., - *La première mission d'Acadie 1603-1616*, Les Presses de l'Université Laval, Cité Universitaire, Québec, 10e, 1967.

Anonymous author - *Conduite des François par rapport à la Nouvelle-Écosse*, Chez les Frères Vaillan, Londres 1755.

Emile Lauvrière - *La Tragédie d'un peuple - Histoire du peuple acadien de ses origines à nos jours*, Éditions Bossard, Paris, 1923.

Antoine Bernard - *Le Drame acadien depuis 1604*, Les Clercs de Saint-Viateur, Montréal, 1936.

Rameau de Saint-Père - *Une colonie féodale en Amérique*. La France aux Colonies, A Jouby, Librairie Editeur, Paris, 1859.

Beamish Murdoch - *A History of Nova Scotia or Acadie, Vol. 1* James Barnes, Printer, Halifax, N.S., 1865.

Public Archives of Canada.

CHAPTER V

Life at Port Royal

In spite of all the conflicts which beset the capital of Acadia during its years under the French Regime, the little colony grew from some 40 people in 1640, to over 400 by 1671, and to 1406 by 1737. It spread throughout the Annapolis Valley, with its greatest concentration from the mouth of the Lequille River to present day Paradise.

The French settlers brought by d'Aulnay were quick to take advantage of the large areas of rich alluvial soil along the banks of the rivers and streams flowing into the Basin.

Among the settlers were "sauniers" from Saintonge and Aunis, who knew how to exploit the salt marshes of those seaside provinces of France. There were others who came from the marshlands of Poitou, who knew how to drain such marshes by ditches. Combining the expertise of both the "sauniers" and the marshland farmers, these pioneers devised the "aboiteau" method of reclaiming large areas of very fertile soil from the tidal waters of the Annapolis Basin, and later of Minas Basin and Beaubassin at the head of the Bay of Fundy.

The "aboiteau" devised by these dykeland farmers consisted of a levee made of tree trunks laid horizontally between other tree trunks driven vertically deep into the ground and covered with heavy clay soil. The levee was not across the mouth of the stream but along the shore, and in order to permit the drainage of the land behind this dyke, they constructed an "aboiteau" which acted as a valve which opened to let the water drain out at low tide, but closed when the tidal water in the river or stream rose against it. This description is taken from Dièreville, who lived at Port Royal in 1700, and left a vivid account of life there.

Once the dyke was completed, two years were allowed for the snow and the rain to wash away the salt deposited on the land over the years. After two years at least, according to Dièreville, these lands produced all the wheat, flax and vegetables the settlers required, and pastured large herds of cattle, sheep and horses. Around this method of cultivating the land, which was peculiar to the French pioneers of Acadia, evolved their dyke land economy, which marked their whole way of life and eventually changed them from Frenchmen to Acadians, a new and distinct ethnic group.

Since this construction and maintenance of the dykes required intense and sustained work at certain times of the year, during the period of low tides, these farmers learned to work together as teams for the common good.

However, once this work was completed, the land produced all they needed without further effort. For that reason, the Acadians, as they became known, cleared little of the uplands, which were not so fertile and so less rewarding for the labour output. As there was little need for land clearing each pioneer family had the opportunity, working as a team, to provide practically all its own requirements for a comfortable, if not luxurious, life in the New World.

The men made all the plain furniture required, tables, chairs, beds, cradles, sideboards (called "dressoir") and benches, from the native wood near at hand. They made the footwear for the whole family, either the wooden shoes (sabots) of their French ancestors or the Indians moccasins, more adapted to Acadian winters. They also had to make their own tools and farm implements, such as wooden plows, hoes, flails, and carts. A young man had to be able to make a wheel before he could think of marrying the girl of his dreams and starting a household of his own.

The women spun the wool from their families' sheep and the flax from their fields, and wove the cloth to dress their families. Dièreville, in his peculiar prose-poetry says: "thus by their own industry, their nudity they cover". This was such an essential part of their way of life that a young girl was not considered eligible for marriage until she could weave a blanket.

As in all frontier communities the men hunted, trapped and fished and also traded with the Indians. Possibly the Acadian men has more time for these pursuits than in other pioneer communities where land clearing required continuous toil. They also found it more convenient and more profitable to trade their surplus furs, fish, meat and wool with New England merchants for manufactured goods than to set up manufactures of their own. Such an economy precludes skilled trades and secondary industries, and the censuses taken in Acadia between 1671 and 1737 bear this out. There were then few tradesmen and no merchants, while practically all heads of households were farmers, owning many cattle, sheep and swine, but having few acres under cultivation. The census of 1671 lists 1 druggist, 3 coopers, 1 weaver, 2 gunsmiths, 1 edged tool maker, 2 carpenters, 1 tailor; all the rest of the 61 heads of families were farmers.

Although these settlers did not specialize in any one trade, they were able to "turn their hand" to many trades. Dièreville describes how they quickly learned to make fishing boats, and to use them to fish in the Annapolis Basin, and to cure this fish, which was as good or superior to the product of a French fishing company that had been exploiting the fisheries of the Bay of Fundy for many years.

The census of 1671 reveals only two carpenters and one mason, yet Dièreville says that whenever a newly married couple needed a house the whole family, brothers and uncles of the bride and groom, would combine their skills to build the future home.

From the few available descriptions, the Acadian house was made from squared logs fitted together at the corners to form a solid rectangular building of modest size. The ordinary home had but one room downstairs, where the family ate and prayed; where the women cooked and spun and rocked the cradle. One corner of this large room was curtained off for the bed of the parents and the baby's cradle. The rest of the children slept in the loft, which was undivided, and served also as a storehouse for the grain; hence the name, "grenier", to indicate this part of the house.

It is very probable that the loom, which was an essential part of each household and which took up much room, would be housed in the "grenier". We may assume this from the practice of the Acadians who settled along the shores of Saint Mary's Bay and elsewhere, to place the large loom in the "grenier", or the upstairs of their house.

Although the poets and romantic writers describe the Acadian dwellings as thatched-roof cottages, it is doubtful if most roofs were covered with that material. It is far more probable that the roofs would be covered with birchbark or with cedar shingles. The Indians would have shown them the adaptability of birchbark to many uses, and the Acadians could well have perceived that if birchbark could make a watertight canoe, it could also make a watertight roof.

As the oldest houses built by the Acadians after their resettlement in Nova Scotia, New Brunswick and elsewhere, were shingled with hand made shingles, one may presume that shingles were used on the Acadian houses in the Annapolis Valley, and elsewhere in Acadia, before 1755. Unfortunately, very few of the Acadian dwellings escaped burning during the Expulsion, and the few that are known to have been still standing when the first Planters came to the area have long since disappeared.

As for the pattern of settlement, both the descriptions left by Dièreville, by the Intendant DeMeulles and the map drawn by Mitchell in 1733, show that the Acadians spread their holdings along the river as far as the ebb and flow of the tides would permit dyke land farming.

Again, according to the above witnesses, Port Royal itself was never settled as a town. From these descriptions only the governor, the soldiers, and five or six inhabitants lived there. The rest had their dwellings on their farms all along the valley. This was a marked departure from the tightly knit villages in their native France, where the peasant dwellings would be grouped around the chateau or around the village square.

The censuses taken between 1671 and 1704 give us an idea of their material wealth and type of agriculture. In 1671 there were 829 cattle, 399 sheep, and 417 acres of cultivated land. This increased to a maximum of 1350 cattle, 1548 sheep, 989 swine and 1610 acres of land suitable for cultivation in 1693. The census of 1707 marks a decrease to 963 cattle, 1245 sheep, 974 swine and 392 3/4 acres of arable land. However, one must remember that 1707 was a very unsettled year, as Port Royal was attacked twice by military expeditions from New England. Both attacks were repulsed by the small garrison with the help of the inhabitants, and this may explain the low acreage under cultivation that year.

These had not been the only setbacks that the colony had had in the past or was to receive in the future. For example, during King William's War or the War of the League of Augsbourg, Port Royal was sacked by the New Englanders under Phipps in 1690, and again by Benjamin Church in 1696.

In 1710 Port Royal fell to a powerful assault led by Colonel Nicholson, and the Acadians had to adjust to a new type of government and a great deal of anxiety under the new regime.

From the minutes of the Council of Annapolis Royal it is evident that there was a good deal of tension between the English governors and the Acadians.

The most contentious issues were forced labour on roads and on the fortifications, the oath of allegiance to the British sovereign, and the denial of exit permits for those who wanted to leave Port Royal for other parts of Acadia, or to go to Isle Royale (Cape Breton) or Isle Saint-Jean (Prince Edward Island), which were French possessions.

The Acadians themselves were torn between their reluctance to leave their fertile lands and happy homes in the Annapolis Valley under English rule, and their desire to live with their compatriots under French rule, in an area devoid of the sunshine and fertility they knew so well.

In the end most of them stayed, and from all accounts they seemed to have reached an understanding with the British authorities, who needed the Acadians to supply the garrison with food, wood and labour.

Under the circumstances the Acadians continued to work their dyked lands and expanded the colony to present day Paradise.

In some ways life was easier for them under the British regime. First of all they no longer had to fear raids from New England expeditions and they could more easily trade with the New England merchants, who now had storehouses at Annapolis. On the other hand the threat of expulsion was always present as long as they refused to take the oath of allegiance. This threat loomed near, in 1720, in 1728-29, and again in 1749, when Cornwallis summoned them to Halifax for that purpose.

But on all these occasions, the stubborn refusal of the Acadians prevailed, and life went on as before in the humble homes along the Annapolis River, from the Bourgeois settlement near Port Wade to Paradise. This pleasant valley with its tidal flats, its climate, and its fertility changed French Poitevin peasants into Acadians, a distinct ethnic group, whose offsprings settled in many other communities that will be the object of the following chapter.

SOURCE OF INFORMATION

Dièreville - *Voyage en Acadie* - Edited by L. U. Fontaine, Québec 1885, pp. 43-67.

Jean-Claude Dupont - "Les défricheurs d'eau" in *Culture vivante*, XXVII, décembre 1972.

Père Clarence J. d'Entremont - *Petit Manuel d'Histoire d'Acadie des Débuts à 1670*, Université de Moncton, 1977, Moncton, N.B.

Nicolas Denys - *Description des Costes de l'Amérique Septentrionale.*

Public Archives of N.S. - *Minutes of His Majesty's Council at Annapolis Royal 1736-1749.*

Andrew Hill Clark - *Acadia, The Geography of Early Nova Scotia to 1760*, The University of Wisconsin Press, Madison, Wis. 1968.

Lucien Campeau, S.J. - *La première mission d'Acadie 1602-1616*, Les Presses de l'Université Laval, Cité Universitaire, Québec, 10e, 1967.

Anonymous author - *Conduite des François par rapport à la Nouvelle-Écosse*,

Chez les Frères Vaillan, Londres 1755.

Emile Lauvrière - *La Tragédie d'un peuple - Histoire du peuple acadien de ses origines à nos jours*, Éditions Bossard, Paris, 1923.

Antoine Bernard - *Le Drame acadien depuis 1604*, Les Clercs de Saint-Viateur, Montréal, 1936.

Rameau de Saint-Père - *Une colonie féodale en Amérique. La France aux Colonies*, A Jouby, Librairie Editeur, Paris, 1859.

Beamish Murdoch - *A History of Nova Scotia or Acadie*, Vol. 1 James Barnes, printer, Halifax, N.S. 1865.

Public Archives of Canada.

1

The Dupuis Family home in the Nova Scotia Museum series, "Les Premières terres acadiennes". Photographs in the following pages are from this same series of watercolours by Azor Vienneau.

2
Acadian Children at play.

3
Using homespun and imported fabrics, Acadians produced clothing that reflected both European traditions and their own lifestyles.

4
Marie-Claire Dupuis spins wool from their sheep to be used for clothing.

5
The Dupuis family garden. Note that their home was destroyed by fire not an uncommon event in those days.

6
An Acadian oven located on the exterior of the house adjacent to the chimney. Access to the oven was gained through the back of the fireplace as shown. The outside cavity was used as a pen for chickens or pigs.

7
As summer draws to a close on the Belleisle marsh, the Dupuis family hosts a gathering of friends and relatives. Thanks are expressed through food, music, and good times.

8
Returning with a load of hay. The cattle were raised primarily for milk and to sell. The principal draft animals were oxen.

CHAPTER VI

Life at Grand Pré, Beaubassin and Other Pre-Expulsion Acadian Communities

Once the best lands in the Annapolis Valley had been taken up by the pioneer families, the sons and grandsons of these families sought similar lands and conditions elsewhere.

The area around Minas Basin offered all the prerequisites for a successful dyke land economy. The numerous rivers and streams flowing into the basin passed through immense tidal flats over which the high tides of the Bay of Fundy deposited each year a rich alluvial soil. The climate was even more attractive than that of the region around Port Royal.

Pierre Melanson and Pierre Theriau seem to have been the leaders in bringing families to the Minas Basin area. The influx of settlers began between 1675 and 1680. The census of 1671 showed no settlers there, but by 1686 there were 10 families, comprising 57 persons, having 90 cattle, 21 sheep, 67 pigs and 83 acres of ploughed land.

Pierre Melanson is usually considered as the founder of Grand Pré, and Pierre Theriau as the first to settle at Rivière des Habitants.

The region around the Basin soon became the hub, so to speak, of the Acadian settlements in Nova Scotia. Other communities grew along the banks of the rivers flowing into the Basin, such as the Rivière des Vieux Habitants, Rivière aux Canards, along the Avon, at Pisiquit, now Windsor and at Cobequid, now Truro.

The population grew slowly at first. The census of 1703 reveals 305 people in the area. Two years later there were 490 persons, and in 1714, the first census taken after the inception of the British regime showed that there were 146 families spread out in six villages on the west side of the Basin. On the east side, at Cobequid, there were 23 families.

However, after this date the population increased very rapidly, while that of the Valley grew more slowly, which might indicate that the Acadians felt that they would have more freedom from the British authorities the further they were from Annapolis. At any rate the census of 1737 showed a very significant increase in population: 2113 persons at Grand-Pré and neighbouring communities and 1623 at Pisiquit (Windsor).

From the description left by DeMeulles in 1686 and from interpretation of the censuses of the period, we may glean a fairly good picture of life in the Grand Pré area before 1755.

As previously noted, most of the men were farmers, with even fewer tradesmen than there were at Port Royal in 1671. Here also, they relied almost entirely on the dyked lands to provide them with wheat, oats, barley, rye, flax and a bountiful crop of hay to feed their herds of cattle, sheep and pigs. Here it is mentioned that undyked lands provided pasture for these same herds. On the uplands, fruit trees provided them with apples, from which they made cider. To embellish their surroundings they also introduced the French willows - these have since spread throughout the region, but are found more in abundance in the area settled by the Acadians.

After the spring work of repairing the old dykes, and building new ones to reclaim more land from the tidal flats, they planted and sowed their crops of wheat, oats, barley, peas, and flax, and tended their flocks and sheared their sheep. During the late summer and early fall they harvested their crops, and later on they killed their surplus animals, cattle, hogs and sheep. They salted what they needed for their winter supply, and exchanged some with the New England merchants who came each year to trade with the Acadians.

From the reports of the British governors at Port Royal and at Halifax, it is apparent that some of their livestock were driven overland to Tatamagouche, and taken thence to Louisbourg. This illegal trade (after 1713) was so widespread as to cause shortages of meat for the British garrison at Port Royal, which also relied on the Acadian's meat and vegetables for its needs.

During the long winters the men and older boys spent most of their time in the woods, cutting firewood or logs for constructing new dwellings, as new homes were going up at a very fast pace, judging from the additional families in each succeeding census. Also judging from the number of guns included in the censuses, one can presume that the men and boys did much hunting and no doubt, some trapping, as furs were exchanged with the Boston merchants, for commodities that they could not produce in this subsistence economy devoid of manufacturing industries.

The older men of the households, who could no longer hunt or work in the woods, fashioned the very plain but practical furniture to satisfy the basic requirements of the household, and made the moccasins which became the most popular footwear among the Acadians. (DeMeulles implies that it was by far the most widely used).

The women and young girls looked after the household, prepared the food from the vegetable gardens in summer, milked the cows, tended the flocks of hens, chicks and geese, and also did their share of the work during the long summer days in the hayfields of the Grand Pré, Port Royal and Beaubassin marshlands.

The women carded, spun and wove the wool from the household's own sheep and also wove into cloth the flax from their fields.

But it was not all work and no play at Grand Pré. In the evenings people would gather at one of the homes among relatives and friends, and sing the songs their forebears had brought from France. They danced their country dances of the provinces of the mother country, and told stories of real or imagined adventures of their ancestors. Also, as Dièreville and Rameau de Saint-Père both say, they talked about their neighbours, as is always the custom among the French.

Also judging from the censuses and from the writings of Bishop Saint-Vallier, Intendant DeMeulles, and Moyse de les Derniers, this was a classless society, for every household depended entirely on its own work for its subsistence.

When differences arose among them, mostly over land ownership, these were put to arbitration before the priest, or before an older inhabitant who had earned unqualified respect from the colonists. Bishop Saint-Vallier mentions in the report of his pastoral visit, that at Grand Pré he spent part of a morning settling disputes among his flock. He also extols their deep faith and their devotion to their two churches at Grand Pré and at Canard.

Another area which attracted the French settlers of Acadia were the vast marshlands of Tantramar, (from the French "tintamare", noise). It was first known as the Bourgeois Colony, from Jacques Bourgeois, the surgeon of Port-Royal, who moved there in 1672 with his two sons-in-laws and their families.

In 1676 all the region between the Petitcodiac and Tatamagouche was given to Michel LeNeuf, Sieur de la Vallières as his "seigneurie", named Beaubassin. One condition of La Vallières, he was not to interfere with the possessions of those already settled there, namely Jacques Bourgeois and his extended family. It seems that La Vallières did try to collect dues from these first settlers but without success.

Beaubassin did not attract a large influx of settlers at first. There were 120 people in 1691, and ten years later, in 1701, there were only 190. The capture of Port Royal seems to have given an impetus to emigrate to this area, as the population increased to 350 in 1714, and to 1816 in 1737.

The intendant DeMeulles who visited here in 1686 left us a good description of the area and of the life of the inhabitants. According to him the Basin (baie de Beaubassin) was a quarter of a league wide at its entrance and extended two leagues inland. (A "league" or "lieue" was the equivalent of 2 1/2 miles). Around this basin was a large area of prairie land on which 100,000 cattle could easily graze. The marshland grass called "misette" was very good to fatten cattle.

DeMeulles mentioned the gently sloping land, covered with hardwood on each side of the tidal flats, where in 1686 there were already 22 farms. The buildings were located on small hills overlooking the flats, and within easy reach of the forest.

DeMeulles remarked that all these inhabitants had three or four buildings in good repair. Most of them had 12 to 15 cattle, 10 to 12 hogs and as many sheep, which remained outside all year except when it was time to butcher them. However, "wild dogs" (wolves) took their toll of the livestock.

DeMeulles noted that they had only a few acres of ploughed land, but he added that when they could cultivate more fields they would have all the wheat they would require, and would not have to import any. This last statement implied that they must have exchanged their surplus animal products to obtain their wheat.

The intendant continued by saying that most of the women wove a kind of muslin cloth (étamine), with which they made clothes for their family. They also wove linen cloth from flax they grew, and knitted all the stockings for the family. Everyone wore homemade moccasins.

Finally DeMeulles remarked that each year an English ship came in during the month of April, and brought them the necessities of life that they could not make themselves; these they got in exchange for the furs they obtained from the Indians. He went on to deplore this trade with the enemy, and advocated that a canal be dug through the Isthmus of Chignecto to enable the merchants from Québec to take advantage of this trade which was going to New England.

A look at the censuses taken during the French Regime shows a steady increase in the number of sheep, cattle and hogs raised, but a great fluctuation in the number of cultivated acres.

After the Treaty of Utrecht in 1713, France still claimed the land north of the Missaquash, a river which crossed the Isthmus of Chignecto. The French agents, especially LeLoutre, the missionary to the Indians, enticed the Acadians living south of the river, in present day Cumberland County, to move north of the river. Many did go, and by 1752 there were 1473 Acadians living in 12 communities in la "Nouvelle-Acadie", present day southeastern New Brunswick. In that year 50 more people had emigrated from Port-Royal and Minas Basin. The census reveals that the new arrivals needed help and would have to receive supplies all year, together with the garrison and government employees numbering 280. The same census also reveals that there were 694 men fit and ready to bear arms.

The military activity around the Isthmus of Chignecto added a new dimension to the way of life of the Acadians in that area. Up to that time, in spite of the turbulent political activity involving Acadia, the Acadians themselves had not been directly involved. Now they were called upon to train and take up arms, in defence of a territory that had become for France a springboard to recapture the territory lost by the Treaty of Utrecht, and a bastion against further penetration by the English into the French areas of North America. They were also called upon to sacrifice their homes at Beaubassin and move across the river to "Nouvelle Acadie". After Beaubassin had thus been evacuated at the insistence of LeLoutre, Indians under his command burned the buildings to prevent any of the Acadians from returning to British soil.

Between 1730 and 1752, many of the former settlers of Beaubassin and Cobequid moved across to Isle Saint-Jean. Here they continued the same type of subsistence and self-sufficient economy that they had practiced at Port Royal, Grand Pré, Cobequid and Beaubassin, but with less success.

By the middle of the eighteenth century the Acadian farmers had had a hundred years of experience in dyke land agriculture, but little training in clearing upland, even the fertile soil of Prince Edward Island. Possibly this lack of training or desire to tackle land clearing, coupled with crop failures due to early frosts and late springs and three invasions of field mice, hindered the agricultural development of the island during the first years.

However the new settlers did take advantage of the abundance of fish in the Gulf of Saint Lawrence, for by 1735 there were 131 of 432 inhabitants classified as fishermen.

After 1749, especially, Isle Saint-Jean received a real influx of settlers from all parts of Acadia. The census taken by de la Rocque in 1752 reveals that there were 2223 persons on the Island. This census also showed that the inhabitants of Isle Saint-Jean were continuing the self-sufficient economy that their forebears had practiced in the older settlements in Acadia.

De la Rocque also stressed that there were five parishes on the island: Saint-Jean l'Evangéliste at Port La Joie (Charlottetown), Holy Family at Malpeque, Saint-Peter at Saint Peters, Saint Louis at Scotchfort, and Saint Paul at Point Prime.

De la Rocque aired his views on the development of the colony, and here some of his comments on the village of Tracadie, which may give an insight on life on the Island in 1752: (translation)

Eight families have settled around the harbour of Tracadie and two at Etang des Berges, three quarters of a league from the said harbour of Tracadie. This place is convenient, as is Saint Pierre harbour, for cod-fishing and farming and the settlers carry on both occupations with equal success.

This harbour is quite large and penetrates two and a half leagues behind the dunes on the east, and a good league inland on the south and retains its full width throughout its entire length.

The inhabitants have settled on the west coast of the harbour, and the lands that they have cleared are partly seeded this year and generally the crop appears quite good. All kinds of trees cover the rest of the upland, while on the east southeast and south south-east there are large prairies with a full hay crop and it would be easy to enlarge them and settle a number of other families here.

The best way to develop the said prairies would be to grant to each inhabitant a sufficient acreage to feed the number of cattle required by each family. If later the family wants to increase its herd it will have to keep on enlarging their lowland in proportion as their livestock increases."

Many Acadians who escaped the Expulsion on the mainland crossed over to Isle Saint-Jean in such numbers that the population doubled in three years, so that by 1756 it was 4400. This influx over-extended the resources of the subsistence economy of the island to such a degree that both the settlers and the newcomers were reduced to extreme poverty, and needed food and clothing from Louisbourg and Quebec.

Three years after the Expulsion from the mainland, the same fate befell the older settlers as well as the newcomers on Isle Saint-Jean. They had to leave in spite of their petition to take the unqualified oath of allegiance. In all, some 3500 Acadians were shipped to France. However, the lack of enough ships left 30 families "stranded" on the island, but these managed to eke out a bare existence all during the period of the Expulsion.

According to Captain Holland, who surveyed the island in 1764, these 30 families were considered prisoners, just like those who were held at Halifax. Holland says they were extremely poor, living in the forest in small cabins that were in very bad condition. These Acadians lived by fishing, and hunting small game, such as rabbits and partridges and even wild cats.

Holland also reports that there were 12,915 cleared acres, 399 houses, 11 mills, 2 churches, and an old fort on Prince Edward Island in 1764. This would give an idea of the extent of settlement on the Island before 1758.

The French government had neglected the settlement of Cape Breton Island, until the Treaty of Utrecht in 1713 deprived it of the mainland of Acadia. But after that date, the French authorities tried to entice as many Acadians as possible to settle on Isle Royale. Some did take up the offer, but Isle Royale did not provide the same advantages as Port Royal, Grand Pré or Beaubassin.

These Acadians settled mostly on Ile Madame and along the southeast coast of Cape Breton. Sieur de la Rocque comments on the condition of these new settlements give us an insight of life there.

Of Ile Madame, de la Rocque said that the land was not easily cultivated, being a clay soil and extremely rocky, heavily forested with a mixture of birch, beech, spruce and fir. The settlers had to pursue many different trades in order to survive. Those who did not fish for cod sailed on coastal ships during the summer, and in winter cut fire wood which they sold at nine "livres" a cord delivered on the coast. He also said that most of the settlers kept a few cattle to supplement their fish diet. De la Rocque added that the coast was suitable for beaching small ships almost anywhere, thereby helping the inshore fishery.

From de la Rocque's census we may easily conclude that fishing was the main occupation of the Acadian settlers on Cape Breton Island. He found 175 fishermen, 37 coastal sailors, 97 farmers, many of whom had little or no cultivated land and few animals, 5 carpenters, 1 surgeon, 21 labourers, 555 fowl and 79 boats. This was by far the largest number of boats reported in any of the Acadian regions. Sieur de la Rocque is rather vague on the cultivated acreage of Cape Breton Island, or Isle Royale. He enumerated only 36 acres as cleared, although he indicates that most of the settlers had a clearing for a vegetable garden. He also mentions numerous "déserts", no doubt marshlands, that were used as pasturage.

Many of the enumerated settlers had only immigrated into the areas during the past three years, since the founding of Halifax. Most of them, and also some who had been there for many years, could not manage a mere subsistence living, because they were all receiving "des vivres du Roy", meaning that they were receiving food from the King's stores at Louisbourg. This must have caused added misery to a group of people who were used to extracting a bountiful food supply from their own land. Here, again, most were living on lands only granted verbally by the proprietors, either officials or merchants at Louisbourg, or by the governor of that city.

If the census takers and intendants and travellers left us fairly precise pictures of the way of life of the Acadians in the Annapolis Valley, around Minas Basin and Beaubassin, on Prince Edward Island and on Cape Breton Island, these same sources were not too eloquent concerning the Acadian settlements in Cape Sable area.

From these censuses and from personal knowledge of the area, it is evident that the early settlers of the Cape Sable area from Pubnico to Cape Sable, through Shag Harbour, Woods Harbour, and Barrington, pursued a subsistence economy based on fishing rather than farming. The censuses reveal a very small acreage of ploughed land, but quite a large number of livestock in proportion to this cleared land, which leads us to believe that they took advantage of the marshlands prevalent in this area for pasture and fodder, but one can well imagine that the rough and rocky terrain from Pubnico to Shelburne would have discouraged large scale land clearing. It is interesting to note the large number of goats and hogs that were kept, probably because these animals can forage and survive on the roughest and poorest vegetation.

If the land was not conducive to the dykeland economy of the other Acadian areas, its numerous inlets and bays were well stocked with shell fish, especially lobsters, and offered safe harbours for small boats to fish on the nearby rich fishing banks.

Later on, especially after 1720, Acadians from Port Royal settled in the Abuptic and Tebok areas (Argyle and Chebogue). Here were large tidal flats that could be dyked by the aboiteau method, and there are remains of such constructions in these areas. Also, when the first English settlers came, they found a large number of cattle still roaming the tidal flats, and some remains of barns and grist mills, which indicated that grain was grown in large enough amounts to warrant more than one such mill.

As the Cape Sable area was closer to New England than any

of the other Acadian communities, a brisk trade went on between the settlers of Cape Sable and the merchants of New England. In fact, the archives of Massachusetts reveal many instances of this illegal trade between two supposedly enemy communities, whose mother countries forbade any foreign trade by their colonies.

Considering the abundance and variety of fish in the waters of southwestern Nova Scotia, coupled with bountiful game, (the fly-path of the migratory water-fowl passes over the area) the large tidal flats and the relatively mild climate, these early settlers must have led an ideal life in tune with the resources that nature provided.

Such was the "modus vivendi" of this ethnic group, the Acadians, who adapted their lifestyle to the land where they lived, instead of trying to change and exploit the environment to suit their whims. They tried not to impoverish either the land or the native people, in order to acquire wealth or power. They let others do the fighting and trading while they extracted from the forest, the tidal flats and the bountiful sea, their food, shelter and clothing and nothing more, as Longfellow so aptly put it:

The richest was poor and the poorest lived in abundance

Moyse de les Derniers summed up perfectly their way of life. In his report on the Acadians just prior to the Expulsion, he says that the Acadians were the most innocent and virtuous people he had known. They lived in perfect equality, without any class distinction. They ignored luxury and comfortable living, for they were content with the simplest way of life which their land provided. Moyse de les Derniers extols their hospitality, their high moral standard, their carefree joy and their unity. To him their way of life typefied the Golden Age.

(Moyse de les Dernier was a Swiss Protestant in the service of Governor Lawrence. His report is in the Public Archives of Nova Scotia).

SOURCES OF INFORMATION

Dièreville - *Voyage en Acadie* - Edited by L.U. Fontaine, Québec 1885, pp. 43-67.

Jean-Claude Dupont - "Les défricheurs d'eau" in *Culture vivante*, XXVII, décembre 1972.

Père Clarence J. d'Entremont - *Petit Manuel d'Histoire d'Acadie des débuts à 1670*, Université de Moncton, 1977, Moncton, N.B.

Nicolas Denys - *Description des Costes de l'Amérique Septentrionale.*

Public Archives of N.S. - *Minutes of His Majesty's Council at Annapolis Royal 1936-1749.*

Andrew Hill Clark - *Acadia, The Geography of Early Nova Scotia to 1760*, The University of Wisconsin Press, Madison, Wis. 1968.

Lucien Campeau, S.J. - *La première mission d'Acadie 1602-1616*, Les Presses de l'Université Laval, Cité Universitaire, Québec, 10e 1967.

Anonymous Authors - *Conduite des François par rapport à la Nouvelle-Écosse*, Chez les Frères Vaillan, Londres 1755.

Emile Lauvrière - La Tragédie d'un peuple - *Histoire du peuple acadien de ses origines à nos jours*, Éditions Bossard, Paris, 1923.

Antoine Bernard - *Le Drame acadien depuis 1604*, Les Clercs de Saint-Viateur, Montréal 1936.

Rameau de Saint-Père - *Une colonie féodale en Amérique - La France aux Colonies*, A Jouby, Librairie Editeur, Paris, 1859.

Beamish Murdoch - *A History of Nova Scotia or Acadia*, Vol. 1 James Barnes, Printer, Halifax, N.S. 1865.

Public Archives of Canada.

CHAPTER VII

Religion and Education in Acadia Before 1755

Religion and education have always been closely allied in Acadia, as indeed in all North America, until well into the present century. But in Acadia before 1755, all education was the responsibility of the church, so it is only logical that both religion and education be considered under the same chapter.

It must be remembered that the letters patent to DeMonts, as well as to Poutrincourt and Razilly, involved christianizing the Indians. Consequently religion was one of the "raison d'être" of Acadia, and so it is not surprising that the religious aspect was always important in the culture of the Acadians.

While DeMonts' and Poutrincourt's colonial associates were comprised of both Protestants and Catholics, it is quite apparent that the colonists who came with Razilly and d'Aulnay all adhered to the Catholic Faith. The few non-Catholics who came to the colony later, such as the Melansons, embraced Catholicism upon marrying Acadian girls.

From the censuses, the parish registers of Port Royal, Grand Pré and Beaubassin, and the reports of the governors and the priests and bishops who visited the area, there seemed to be but one faith in Acadia.

Dièreville described the church at Port Royal as a very unpretentious building, not very different from any other building. He said that he would have mistaken it for a barn, rather than a temple of God, and the priest himself lived in a very sparsely-furnished room in the rear of the same building. This would indicate that the Acadians were not prone to manifest their religion by pretentious buildings, for theirs seemed to have been more a religion of deep inner convictions.

Bishop St. Valliers described the spiritual aspect of the people of Grand Pré and Pisiquid thus: (translation)

The inhabitants are mostly young people, well-built and hard-working, who came from Port Royal. I spent a whole day just to

satisfy their intense devotion. In the morning I heard their confessions, celebrated Mass, gave them communion; and in the afternoon I baptized a number of children and settled some minor differences among the families.
They all insisted on having a resident priest for whom they would provide all the necessary food and lodging, and also wanted to build a chapel and a house for him on the property belonging to one of them.

Of those at Beaubassin, Bishop St. Valliers says:

During the short time we spent with you we were edified by the zeal which you manifest for your religion, by the faithfulness you have in providing for your missionaries for whom you have also erected a small chapel. There is every reason to hope that with a seigneur as faithful and as pious as yours, you will soon have a real church. (Seigneur referred to was de la Vallieres).

Father Petit of Port Royal wrote to Mgr. de St. Valliers about his parishioners:

One hears no swearing, nor does one see any drunkenness or debauchery, and even though they are spread over four or five leagues from the church they all attend mass on Sundays and on holidays.

These were not just polite compliments to a primitive people, for Mgr. de St. Valliers on occasion, did not mince words, as in his admonitions to the people of Gaspé. There he deplores "so little peace, so little unity, in observance of Sunday, stealing of fishing gear, drunkenness, and debauchery of Indians with fire water".

Thus we have a picture of a deeply religious people living in a pastoral setting. During the French regime in Acadia about 40 priests came from France to Acadia as pastors and missionaries. They were at the same time ministers of God, directors of conscience, political guides, and arbitrators and judges in the difficulties that arose among their flocks, because the local government officials under the French regime were often inefficient and corrupt, and the English were reluctant to hear their cases, as the Acadians were not considered British subjects.

However they were not blindly subservient to their clergy. We have seen that Charles de La Tour and his men kept on their irregular lives with the Indian women in spite of the missionaries, and that Biencourt and his men had their differences with the Jesuits. Also, in spite of the admonitions of the missionaries, the frontier seigneurs and governors kept furnishing the Indians with "firewater".

The Acadians themselves showed their independence towards their priests. At Grand Pré and Beaubassin it was the people themselves who told the Bishop they would support a missionary and build a chapel, and not the Bishop who decided when and where a chapel would be built with directives to support the missionary. Too, when the inhabitants of Beaubassin thought that their missionary was spending too much time with the Indians and not enough time in the parish, they were not afraid to complain to the Bishop, saying they would not support their priest unless he gave up his unacceptable behaviour. The missionary complied with their wishes after being admonished by the Bishop, who supported the stand of his Acadian flock and promised them more priests.

The pre-Expulsion Acadians therefore appear as a deeply religious people, staunchly Roman Catholic, with a certain spirit of independence toward religious authority as toward all authority. This was due in part to the scarcity of religious personnel to serve such a large territory.

Nevertheless their faith must have been strongly anchored to survive the storm of the Expulsion, when they were thrown in among people of a strong alien faith, and they themselves were absolutely without the spiritual guidance of their own faith from 1755 to 1769; and even up to 1800, their contacts with religious authority were few and far between. Yet they remained steadfast to their faith and never, as a group, accepted any other, although under the circumstances it would have been so easy to do.

Unfortunately, this strong faith was marred by the proneness to superstition, and a tenacious stubbornness which often hindered their prosperity.

Education

Closely allied with their religion was their education. We find, if we examine things closely, that they compared favourably with other colonists of the same period.

Starting in 1633, the Capuchin Fathers had a school at La Have. This was two years before the founding of the Seminary at Quebec and four years before the founding of Harvard.

After the colony was transferred to Port Royal, 12 Capuchin Fathers directed a seminary where instruction was given to about 30 French and as many Indian boys. The governess of d'Aulnay's children, Mme de Brice, taught both French and Indian girls.

It was in the seminary of Port Royal that the first two Acadian priests, Bernardin and René de Gannes, began their studies.

In 1684 a girls' school was opened in Port Royal by the Sisters of the Congregation of Notre-Dame from Montréal.

In 1701, Sister Chausson of the Congregation of the Cross became the directress of this school. There were also schools at Grand Pré and Beaubassin.

When studying old documents of the period wherein there are signatures of Acadians, we find that about 60% of them could sign their names while the remainder "put their marks". This indicated a fairly high literacy rate for the period.

In 1766 four young men, from exiled Acadian families completed their studies in a seminary in France. They were from Grand Pré, where they had received their elementary education. Two of them returned to America after ordination - one, Mathurin Bourg, became missionary to the Acadians in Nova Scotia, while Jean-Baptiste Breau became pastor to the Acadians settled at St. Jacques de l'Achigan in Quebec.

It was following the Expulsion that education among the Acadians practically disappeared for a full half century.

SOURCES OF INFORMATION

Antonio Dragon - *L'Acadie et ses 40 Robes noires* - Bellarmin, Montréal 1973.

L'Abbé Azaire Couillard -Després - *En marge de la tragédie d'un peuple*, d'Emile Lauvirère, *Observations, sur l'Histoire de l'Acadie Française* de M. Moreau, Paris 1873, Montréal 1919. *Charles de Saint-Etienne de La-Tour au tribunal* de *l'histoire. Charles de St. Etienne de La Tour et son temps 1593-1666.*

Père Clarence J. d'Entremont - *Petit Manuel d'Histoire d'Acadie des débuts à 1670.* Université de Moncton, 1977, Moncton, N.B.

Nicolas Denys - *Description des Costes de l'Amérique Septentrionale.*

Emile Lauvrière - *La Tragédie d'un peuple - Histoire du peuple acadien de ses origines à nos jours*, Éditions Bossard, Paris, 1923.

Antoine Bernard - *Le Drame acadien depuis 1604*, Les Clercs de Saint-Viateur, Montréal, 1936.

Rameau de Saint-Père - *Une colonie féodale en Amérique - La France aux Colonies*, A Jouby, Librairie Editeur, Paris, 1859.

Beamish Murdoch - *A History of Nova Scotia or Acadia*, Vol. 1 James Barnes, Printer, Halifax, N.S. 1865.

Lucien Campeau, S.J. - *La première mission d'Acadie 1602-1616.* Les Presses de l'Université Laval, Cité Universitaire, Québec, 10e, 1967.

Public Archives of Nova Scotia, Halifax, N.S.

Public Archives of Canada, Ottawa, Canada.

CHAPTER VIII

The Acadian Family

As far as can be ascertained from available documents the first European families, consisting of man and wife and children, to come to Acadia arrived on the south shore of Nova Scotia between 1632 and 1636.

While it is true that Claude de La Tour came to Port Royal in either 1606 or 1607 with his fourteen year old son, Charles, there is no mention of the mother being with them. The same is true of Poutrincourt and his son Charles de Biencourt.

Claude de La Tour brought his second wife to Cape Sable in 1630 under rather adverse conditions, which were described by Nicolas Denys in *Description des Costes de l'Amérique Septentrionel*, Paris.

According to Denys, Claude de La Tour had been captured by the Kirke Brothers on the high seas in 1629 and taken to England where he married a lady-in-waiting to Queen Henrietta, daughter of the King of France. While in England, Claude de La Tour had become a British subject and had accepted from Sir William Alexander a baronetcy comprising all the Cape Sable area. The grant and titles were for himself and his son. Claude then came to Fort Saint-Louis, backed by an armed escort, to persuade his son to accept the British offer and renounce his allegiance to the King of France. This meant passing over to England the last foothold that France still held in North America. The Kirke brothers had already captured Quebec and all the other French posts along the coast of Acadia. Charles resisted both the honours offered by his father and the armed attack by the Scottish escort. After this failure to secure the stronghold, Claude de La Tour felt it was safer to seek asylum with his son than to return to England, or with the Scots at Charles Fort. Charles granted his father's request for asylum for himself, his wife and two women servants, but would not permit them to set foot inside his fort. According to Denys, Claude and his wife and servants were still living there in a comfortable house outside the fort when he, Denys, passed there in 1636.

At the same time Charles de La Tour had a family of his own with his Indian wife, Marie. This union had been blessed by the Recollet missionaries who came to Acadia between 1616 and 1624. There were at least three children from this marriage. The oldest girl, Jeanne, married Martin d'Apprendestiguy, sieur de Martignon. The other two were placed in a convent in France at Beaumont-les-Tours. One died quite young and the other, Antoinette, took her religious vows in 1646.

Speaking of the colony at La Have, Nicolas Denys mentions ten or fifteen "tenanciers" (land holders) and says that his commander Razilly "has no other desire than to increase the population of the country and that every year he brings people in to realize this aim". This would imply that families were brought in. Unfortunately the passenger lists of ships leaving France for the colony of La Have have not been found for the period of 1632 to 1635.

The passenger list of the °Saint Jehan° which left France for Acadia on April 1st, 1636, reveals a number of families, some of whom appear in the census of Port Royal of 1671.

From a memo by the Capuchins in 1644 telling what d'Aulnay had done we read:

That he maintained two hundred men, soldiers, labourers, craftsmen, and also women and children, Capuchins and Indian children. Moreover there are twenty French households that are here, families that will people the country in which the Sieur d'Aulnay would bring many others if he had the means.

From what part of France did these families come?

Dr. Genevieve Massignon in a book *Les Parlers Français d'Acadie,* has researched the coincidence between the names of families of Port Royal in the first census of Acadia in 1671, and the families on the lands of d'Aulnay at Martaizé and at La Chaussée, near Loudun, Dept. of Vienne, France and found many of the same names.

It is logical to presume that the first families to take root in Acadia came with Razilly and d'Aulnay, and with de La Tour between 1632 and 1636. Then d'Aulnay recruited families among his tenant farmers in France between 1640 and 1650. There does not seem to have been any immigration from France between 1650 and 1670, during the British occupation. Then in 1670, the ship l'Oranger brought more families.

We should mention here that the Acadians developed a clan system in the New World. Each extended family formed a village or a clan around the holdings of the first one bearing that family name to settle in the area. The same pattern of family grouping was evident in their resettlement in Nova Scotia, for in most Acadian villages one Acadian family name predominates, as for example, the Deveaus in Salmon River, and the d'Entremonts in West Pubnico.

SOURCES OF INFORMATION

Geneviève Massignon - *Les parlers français d'Acadie* - Tome I, Librairie C. Klincksieck, Paris.

Le Rolle du "Saint Jehan", Archives Publiques du Canada.

Les Notes généalogiques de Placides Gaudet, Archives Publiques du Canada.

Régistres des paroisses de Beaubassin et de Port Royal, copies des originaux au Centre Acadien de l'Université Sainte-Anne.

CHAPTER IX

Events Leading to the Expulsion

The Treaty of Utrecht, signed on April 11, 1713, really started the chain of events which led to the removal of the Acadians from Acadia. By this treaty, King Louis XIV of France very reluctantly renounced all his claims to Acadia "dans ses anciennes limites", which could be translated "inside its former boundaries".

During the next forty years diplomats from both Great Britain and France wrangled over the question of the former boundaries of Acadia without ever arriving at a solution; and both sides were convinced that only force of arms would solve the problem. France claimed that the former limits of Acadia comprised only the area of mainland Nova Scotia, granted to Charles de La Tour in 1638, in addition to the region of Port Royal; while the British argued that the former boundaries of Acadia took in all of the present province of New Brunswick and what is now the State of Maine, in addition to all of mainland Nova Scotia. Both countries agreed that Isle Saint-Jean (Prince Edward Island) and Isle Royale (Cape Breton Island) were not included within the boundaries of Acadia.

The terms of the treaty gave the Acadians the choice to either leave the province with their belongings and go to any place they wished, within a year, or to remain in Acadia as British Subjects, enjoying "the free exercise of their religion according to the usage of the Church of Rome as far as the laws of Great Britain do allow the same".

The status of the Acadians is redefined by a letter from Queen Anne to Nicholson, June 23, 1713...

Signifie Our Will and Pleasure to you that you permit and allow such of them as have any lands or Tenements in the Places under your Government in Acadie and Newfoundland, that have been or are to be yielded to Us by Vertue of the late Treaty of Peace, and are Willing to Continue our Subjects to retain and

Enjoy their said Lands and Tenements without any Lett or Molestation as fully and freely as other our Subjects do or may possess their Lands and Estates or to sell the same if they shall rather Chuse to remove elsewhere...

On her part, France would have liked the Acadians to leave mainland Nova Scotia and settle on Isle Saint-Jean, or Isle Royale, or north of the Isthmus of Chignecto. An influx of Acadians, who were already used to the country, to these areas retained by France would greatly increase the strength and prosperity of these French colonies, and at the same time so weaken the newly acquired British colony that it would become an easy prey to the perennial enemy (France) in any future conflict.

The Acadians let it be known that they would leave rather than take an oath of allegiance to Queen Anne. Consequently they sent delegates, as was their custom, to inspect the land that France offered to them. They returned less than enthusiastic about the prospect of settling in Cape Breton, where they found the soil and climate very unsuitable. Isle Saint-Jean was more promising but the move involved great sacrifices, and the disruption of a way of life that had become part and parcel of their culture. While a few decided to leave, the great majority decided to remain and wait and see if the British governors would force the hated oath on them or persecute them for their religion.

Not only were they not pressed to take the oath, but even those who wanted to leave were prevented from doing so by a series of petty schemes, such as refusing permission to French vessels from Isle Royale to come to Port Royal to embark the Acadians, and forbidding English vessels to sail to French territories. The British governors realized the precarious position of their colony if the Acadians left the territory. Not only the neighbouring potential enemy Country would be greatly strengthened, but Acadia would be left without its agricultural industry and its farmers to provision the garrisons. Moreover the Indians would either leave with the Acadians or become more hostile. In either case the British fur traders in Nova Scotia would lose.

In 1714 Queen Anne died and was succeeded by George I. Thomas Cauldfield, who had succeeded Nicholson as lieutenant-governor, decided to test the Acadians again on the question of the oath, as it was customary to swear allegiance to a new sovereign. The Acadians made it clear that they would not take the oath unless they were exempted from military service. It was the first statement of their policy of neutrality. Again, the British did not force them to depart.

In 1717, the French started work on the fortress of Louisbourg. This was seen as a menace to the British possession of Acadia. John Doucett, who had succeeded Cauldfield as lieutenant-governor, tried to obtain an unqualified oath of allegiance from the inhabitants. This time a new element entered the picture. The Indians, upon hearing of the pressure to take the oath, warned the Acadians that if they did take this oath they would be considered as their enemies, and would suffer the most unpleasant reprisals.

The Indians, who had been most friendly towards the Acadians, now started to threaten them if they appeared too cooperative with the British. Some inhabitants, such as René LeBlanc of Grand Pré and Prudent Robichaud of Port Royal, were threatened and even physically abused by Indians, because they held positions of trust with the British authorities.

The Acadians offered to take an oath of allegiance, provided they were exempt from taking arms against the French or the Indians. Also, for the first time, the Acadians asked the services of British troops to protect them against the Indians, who now frequently attacked British property in the province. The British authorities accused the Acadians of disloyalty for not warning them of these raids, and the Indians threatened to scalp the Acadians if they did warn the authorities. (From Minutes of His Majesty's Council at Annapolis and Petitions of the Acadians to the Great and General Court of Massachusetts.)

In 1720, Colonel Richard Philipps arrived as governor, and called upon the Acadians to take an unqualified oath of allegiance or to leave the country within four months, without the right to sell or dispose of their property and to take only two sheep per family with them. Again the Acadians refused, saying that such an oath would bring the Indians upon them. They again asked for protection from the Indians if they took a qualified oath, and received no reply to their request. The truth of the matter was that even if the governor had wished to grant them the protection, he did not have enough troops to police the extensive territory now occupied by the Acadians. Governor Philipps did not press the matter further, so the great majority of the Acadians remained, but some became uneasy and left for Isle Saint-Jean, Isle Royale and for Tebok and Abuptic in Southwestern Nova Scotia. The census of de la Rocque in 1752 indicates that there were people from Port Royal and Grand Pré at Isle Saint-Jean and Isle Madame since 1720. Father C. d'Entremont speaks of an immigration to Tebok and Abuptic from 1720 on.

In 1727, Ensign Wroth obtained an oath from the people of Minas and Beaubassin which can be summed up as follows: "I promise and swear sincerely, that I shall be entirely faithful and will obey fully His Majesty, King George II and that I recognize Him as the Sovereign of Acadia or Nova Scotia. So help me God." Ensign Wroth had promised them in writing the following: freedom in the exercise of their religion, exemption from bearing arms, and liberty to withdraw from the province at any time. Armstrong, who was acting governor at the time, rebuked the officer for his actions and declared the promises void. Furthermore, when the inhabitants of Annapolis offered to take the same oath, their delegates were cast in jail. However, upon Governor Philipps' return they were released, and another oath was administered to them and to the people of Minas Basin.

The Acadians became known as French Neutrals. Neutrality, in fact became the cornerstone of their policy in relations with both their English rulers and their French neighbouring colonies. (Naomi Griffiths, *The Acadians, Creation of a People.* Ch. II)

They felt that the policy was reasonable and just, and that they had the right to adopt and follow it. Unfortunately for them, neither the English authorities in Nova Scotia and Massachusetts, nor the French at Beauséjour and Louisbourg accepted this view.

The neutrality of the Acadians was severely tested from 1744 to 1748, during the War of the Austrian Succession. In 1744 Duvivier attempted to recapture Port Royal. He left Louisbourg with 990 militiamen and captured Canso, guarded by a handful of British soldiers, then proceeded to Beaubassin and Baie Verte, thence to Annapolis. Cannons were to be sent from Louisbourg by sea, but they arrived too late. L'abbé LeLoutre had left before Duvivier from Beaubassin with 300 Indians,,, but had turned back after a few skirmishes around Annapolis and Bloody Ridge. The Acadians in general did not take part in these two expeditions, but some had furnished supplies to Duvivier, thereby casting suspicion on the whole population. The following year, Capt. Paul Marin with 200 militiamen and 40 Indians attacked Port Royal. As it is impossible to take a fort without cannons the attack failed. He nevertheless captured two merchant ships and their cargo in the harbour, but he was suddenly recalled with his troops to defend Louisbourg under siege.

Louisbourg fell to the New Englanders after a two-month battle. The capture of Louisbourg was a great humiliation to France, who thought the fortress was impregnable. It became a matter of national pride for the government of that country to recapture not only Louisbourg, but also all of Acadia.

France armed a strong fleet to recapture both Louisbourg and Port Royal. It was beset with misfortunes from the start. Its commander, D'Anville, had never been to sea, so it was ill-fitted out and badly provisioned. Sickness carried off hundreds shortly after leaving France, and violent storms drove half the fleet either to Sable Island or to the West Indies. The rest landed in Chebucto Harbour (Halifax), where a thousand more died, including D'Anville and his vice-admiral. The third in command, LaJonquière, set out with the remainder of the fleet to attack Annapolis but another storm off Cape Sable forced him to return to France.

In the winter of 1747, 500 New England soldiers under the command of Colonel Arthur Noble were quartered at Grand-Pré. Although the people of the village had warned him of the possibility of an attack by a troop of French-Canadian militiamen, stationed at Beaubassin under DeRamesay, the English commander ignored the warning, confident that the severe winter weather would make such a trek from Beaubassin impossible. Nevertheless on January 21, 240 Quebecers and 20 Indians set out from Beaubassin. They arrived at Grand Pré on February 10, guided by some young Acadians, and attacked the sleeping soldiers. After 36 hours of bloody fighting, the New England troops surrendered and were allowed to withdraw to Annapolis, bringing their dead, among whom were Colonel Noble and five of his officers.

All these attacks by the French to retake Acadia did not help the position of the neutral Acadians, although Paul Mascarene made it clear in his letters to the home government that without the neutrality of the Acadians it would have been impossible to defend the territory of Nova Scotia. To add to the distrust, Louisbourg was returned to France in 1748 by the treaty of Aix-la-Chapelle. This further aggravated the hatred against the Acadians, and made the New Englanders and William Shirley, governor of Massachusetts, in particular, more determined than ever to rid the province of the French.

In 1749, the British founded Halifax to counter the threat of Louisbourg, now returned to France. That year, 2,500 English settlers were landed at Halifax, and the capital of Nova Scotia was moved from Annapolis to the new town.

Three Acadian delegates from Minas came to Halifax in July

to present their respects to Col. Edward Cornwallis, and were presented with a proclamation ordering them to take the unqualified oath of allegiance by October 15, or forfeit all their rights and possessions in Nova Scotia. Their reaction to this demand was the same as before: they would agree to take an oath which exempted them from bearing arms against the French and Indians, otherwise they would leave the province. Governor Cornwallis did not press the matter further.

To counteract Halifax, the French began to fortify their positions on the isthmus of Chignecto, and put pressure on the Acadians to leave Nova Scotia and move to the north side of the Missaquash River. In the spring of 1750, some Acadians asked permission to leave the province, but Cornwallis refused to grant their requests, saying that they would have to wait until "peace and tranquility are re-established in the Province".

During that year, both the British and the French manoeuvered for positions on the isthmus. L'abbé LeLoutre, missionary to the Indians, persuaded the Acadians of Beaubassin to cross over to the north side of the Missaquash. After Beaubassin was evacuated the Micmac Indians, commanded by LeLoutre, burned the buildings to prevent the return of the Acadians, and to discourage the British troops from moving into a deserted area. Nevertheless, in the fall, Colonel Lawrence began to build Fort Lawrence on the site of Beaubassin, and Luc de la Corne, the commander of the French forces, pushed on with the construction of Fort Beauséjour and Fort Gaspéreau.

Peregrine Hopson replaced Cornwallis in 1752, and during his administration from 1752 to 1754, the Acadians enjoyed a good rapport with the governor, and the colony prospered. Hopson also maintained good relations with the governor of Louisbourg, but unfortunately for the Acadians, Hopson had to leave his post due to ill-health, and Colonel Lawrence replaced him as lieutenant-governor.

Lawrence was convinced that the French, using Beauséjour as a base, were going to attack Nova Scotia, and persuaded Governor Shirley of Massachusetts to send a force of 2,000 New England volunteers, commanded by Monckton and Winslow to attack Fort Beauséjour.

The threat from the French at Beauséjour and Gaspéreau had been exaggerated for the fort was undermanned and in no state to withstand a siege. According to Winslow himself, Fort Gaspéreau was in a pitiful state when it surrendered.

Fort Beauséjour was besieged on June 2, 1755 and surrendered on June 16. Some 400 Acadians were found among the garrison, and Lawrence used this fact as a proof that the Acadians could not be trusted not to take up arms, although the French Commander, Duchambon de Vergor, had vouched that he had forced them under pain of death to take up arms in defence of the fort. Colonel Monckton accepted Vergor's statement and "pardoned" the Acadian defenders.

Meanwhile, a force of British soldiers had raided Grand Pré and seized a quantity of arms and ammunition in the homes of the villagers. Later that month all the Acadians in Nova Scotia were ordered to surrender their firearms or to be treated as rebels. They complied with the order, but later petitioned the governor to rescind his order, as they were left without recourse against the wild animals that were damaging their crops.

In July the Acadians sent delegates to Halifax to request the return of their arms. They were told that they must take an unqualified oath of allegiance, but they refused and were imprisoned. A second group of delegates replied to lieutenant-governor Lawrence on July 25, that they could not take an oath of allegiance that did not exempt them from bearing arms. These, too, were cast into prison and Lawrence sent out the following proclamation to the commanders at Beauséjour, Piziquid and Annapolis:

GOVERNOR LAWRENCE TO COL. MONCKTON

HALIFAX, 31 JULY, 1755

The deputies of the French inhabitants of the districts of Annapolis, Mines and Piziquid, have been called before the council, and have refused to take the oath of allegiance to his Majesty, and have also declared this to be the sentiments of the whole people, whereupon the council advised and it is accordingly determined that they shall be removed out of the country as soon as possible, and as to those about the Isthmus who were in arms and therefore entitled to no favour from the government it is determined to begin with them first; and for this purpose orders are given for a sufficient number of transports to be sent up the Bay with all possible dispatch for taking them on board, by whom you will receive particular instructions as to the manner of their being disposed of, the places of their destination and every other thing necessary for that purpose.

In the mean time, it will be necessary to keep this measure as secret as possible, as well to prevent their attempting to escape, as to carry off their cattle etc.; and the better to effect this you will endeavour to fall upon some stratagem to get the men, both young and old (especially the heads of families) into your power and detain them till the transports shall arrive, so as that they may be ready to be shipped off; for when this is done it is not much to be feared that the women and children will attempt to go away and carry off the cattle. But least they should, it will not only be very proper to secure all their shallops, boats, canoes and every other vessel you can lay your hands upon; but also to send out parties to all suspected roads and places from time to time, that they may be thereby intercepted. As their whole stock of cattle and corn is forfeited to the crown by their rebellion, and must be secured & apply'd towards a reimburse-

ment of the expense the government will be at in transporting them out of the country, care must be had that nobody make any bargain for purchasing them under any colour or pretence whatever; if they do the sale will be void, for the inhabitants have now (since the order in council) no property in them, nor will they be allowed to carry away the least thing but their ready money and household furniture.

The officers commanding the fort Piziquid and the garrison of Annapolis Royal have nearly the same orders in relation to the interior inhabitants. But I am informed those will fall upon the ways and means in spite of all our vigilance to send off their cattle to the island of St. John & Louisbourg (which is now in a starving condition) by the way of Tatamagouche. I would therefore, have you without loss of time, send thither a pretty strong detachment to beat up that quarter and to prevent them. You cannot want a guide for conducting the party, as there is not a Frenchman in Chignecto but must perfectly know the road.

Chas. Lawrence

An uneasy calm prevailed in the villages during the summer, while unbeknown to the Acadians, Mr. Saul of Halifax was chartering ships in New England for the eventual transportation of the whole Acadian population to the thirteen Colonies.

Winslow and his troops moved into the Grand Pré region and occupied the church grounds, and on September 2, they ordered all the men and the boys ten years old and over to come to the church within three days. On September 5, the 418 assembled Acadians heard the following Proclamation:

"GENTLEMEN; I have received from his Excellency, Governor Lawrence, the King's Commission which I have in my hand, and by whose orders you are Conveyed together, to Manifest to you His Majesty's final resolution to the French inhabitants of this, his Province of Nova Scotia, who for almost half a century have had more Indulgence Granted them than any of his

Subjects in any part of his Dominions. What use you have made of them you yourself Best Know.

"The Part of Duty I am now upon is what thot Necessary is Very Disagreeable to my natural make and Temper, as I know it Must be Grievous to you who are of the Same Specia.

"But it is not my business to annimadvert, but to obey Such orders as I receive, and therefore without Hesitation Shall Deliver you his Majesty's orders and Instructions, Vist.:

"That your Lands & Tennements, Cattle of all Kinds and Live Stock of all Sorts are Forfeited to the Crown with all other your Effects Saving your money and Household Goods, and you your Selves to be removed from this his Province.

"Thus it is Preremptorily his Majesty's orders That the whole French inhabitants of these Districts be removed and I am Throh his Majesty's Goodness Directed to allow you Liberty to Carry your money and Household Goods as Many as you Can without Discommoding the Vessels you Go in. I shall do Every thing in my Power that all Those Goods be Secured to you and that you are Not Molested in Carrying of them of, and also that Whole Family Shall go in the Same Vessel, and make this remove, which I am Sensable must give you a great Deal of Trouble, as Easy as his Majesty's Service will admit, and hope that in what Ever part of the world you may Fall you may be faithful Subjects, a Peasable and happy People.

"I Must also Inform you That it is his Majesty's Pleasure that you remain in Security under the Inspection and Direction of the Troops that I have the Honr. to Command."

The removal did not proceed as smoothly as planned. At Grand-Pré and Beaubassin all the chartered vessels did not arrive on time. Some of the detained Acadians escaped at all three principal locations, Annapolis, Minas Basin and Beaubassin. Although Winslow had promised not to separate the families, many separations occurred, and the transports were so overcrowded that the poor exiles could not take even the barest necessities for survival in a foreign land.

Winslow has left the following description of the embarkation:

"Began to embark the inhabitants who went off solentarily and unwillingly, the women in great distress carrying off their children in their arms: others carrying their decrepit parents in their carts, with all their goods, moving in great confusion, and appeared a scene of woe and distress."

According to Winslow, 2,242 persons were deported from Grand-Pré and Piziquid. A church, 11 mills, 276 barns and 255 houses were burned. At Annapolis, 1664 persons were put aboard transports, but it was estimated that some 300 escaped to the woods. Most of the settlers at Cobequid escaped, either to Isle Saint-Jean or to Isle Royale, while at Beaubassin many more fled to the woods, and some carried on a guerilla warfare against the troops of Captain Scott until the fall of Louisbourg in 1758, while others only surrendered after the fall of Quebec.

According to the plan of the Deportation, 2000 were destined to Massachusetts, 700 to Connecticut, 300 to New York, 500 to Maryland, 500 to North Carolina, 500 to South Carolina, 400 to Georgia and 1000 to Virginia.

Many did not reach their destination. The mortality rate appears to have been high on the sea voyages. Two of the ships were driven to San Domingo, where the Acadians were abandoned, whence they either made their way to France or to Louisiana. One ship sank in a storm and one, the Pembroke, was captured by the Acadians and sailed to the Saint John River, from whence the exiles made their way to Quebec. At any rate the number of Acadians found in each of the colonies in 1763 was far less than the above figures.

Deportations continued throughout the period of the Seven Years War, (known as the French and Indian Wars in America), from Southwestern Nova Scotia and from Isle Saint-Jean and Isle Royale. In all, it is estimated that some 14,000 people were uprooted from their homes throughout Atlantic Canada from 1755 to 1763. Some of them remained displaced persons for some 30 years, as the last migration of Acadians from France to Louisiana occurred in 1785.

The Expulsion was a traumatic event for the Acadian ethnic group and one which had profound repercussions. Such an event deserves that its causes be carefully examined, which will be the object of the following chapter.

APPENDIX

Some pertinent documents to the Deportation from the Public Archives of Nova Scotia and the Public Archives of Canada.

GOVERNOR LAWRENCE TO BOARD OF TRADE

HALIFAX, 18th July, 1755

My Lords.-

Since my last, of 28th of June 1755, sent express by Lieutenant Cunningham, the French have abandoned their Fort at St. John's River and, as far as it was in their power, demolished it. As soon as the Forts upon the Isthmus were taken, Captain Rous sailed from thence with three twenty Gun Ships, and a Sloop, to look into St. John's River, where it was reported there were two French Ships of Thirty-six Guns each; he anchored off the mouth of the River, and sent in his boats to reconnoitre; they found no ships there, but, on their appearance, the French burst their Cannon, blew up their Magazine, burned everything they could, belonging to the Fort, and marched off. The next morning, the Indians invited Captain Rous on shore, gave him the strongest assurances of their desire to make peace with us, and pleaded in their behalf, that they had refused to assist the French upon this occasion, tho' earnestly pressed by them. I ex-

pect some of their Chiefs here in a very few days.

As the French Inhabitants of this Province have never yet, at any time, taken the oath of allegiance to His Majesty, unqualified, I thought it my duty to avail myself of the present occasion, to propose it to them; and, as the deputies of the different districts in Mines Basin, were attending in Town upon a very insolent Memorial, they had delivered to the Council, I was determined to begin with them. They were accordingly summoned to appear before the Council, and, after discussing the affair of the Memorial, article by article, the oath was proposed to them; they endeavoured, as much as possible, to evade it, and at last desired to return home and consult the rest of the Inhabitants, that they might either accept or refuse the Oath in a body; but they were informed that we expected every man upon this occasion to answer for himself, and as we would not use any compulsion or surprise, we gave them twenty four hours time to deliver in their answer; and, if they should then refuse, they must expect to be driven out of the country; and tho' they should afterwards repent of their refusal, they would not be permitted to take the oath. The next morning, they appeared and refused to take the oath without the old reserve of not being obliged to bar arms, upon which, they were acquainted, that as they refused to become English subjects, we could no longer look upon them in that light; that we should send them to France by the first opportunity, and till then, they were ordered to be kept prisoners at George's Island, where they were immediately conducted. They have since earnestly desired to be admitted to take the oath, but have not been admitted, nor will any answer be given them until we see how the rest of the Inhabitants are disposed.

I have ordered new Deputies to be elected, and sent hither immediately, and am determined to bring the Inhabitants to a compliance, or rid the province of such perfidious subjects. Your Lordships will see our proceedings in this case at large, as soon as it is possible to prepare minutes of Council.

I am, & C.

ORDERS & INSTRUCTIONS TO MAJOR PREBBLE

By His Excelly. Charles Lawrence Esq. & c., &c., &c.

To Major Prebble commanding the Battalion of Major General Shirley's New England Regiment now embarked in this Harbour in order for their Return to Boston.

Whereas the Government of this Province on account of their having refused to take the oath of Allegiance to his Majesty, and given instances of treasonable & treacherous behaviour on their Parts; and Whereas Orders were accordingly issued for the removal of said Inhabitants, not-withstanding which I have been informed that some of them do still remain in different parts of the province, particularly at Cape Sable and the places round about. You are therefore hereby required & directed to put into Cape Sable, or some of the adjacent Harbours (in your way to Boston) and with the Troops under your command, to land at the most convenient place; and to Seize as many of the said inhabitants as possible, & carry them with you to Boston, where you will deliver them to his Ex. gov. Shirley, with a letter you will receive with the order. You are at all events to burn & destroy the Houses of the said Inhabitants, & carry their utencils & cattle of all kinds, and make a distribution of them to the Troops under your Command as a Reward for the performance of this Service, & to destroy such things as cannot conveniently be carried off. Given under my hand & seal at Halifax this 9 April 1756.

CHAS. LAWRENCE

By his Excellys Command.
WM. COTTRELL

SOURCES OF INFORMATION

Public Archives of Canada - correspondence of William Shirley, Charles Lawrence, Jonathan Belcher, Paul Mascarene, Montague Wilmot, Colonel Winslow, The Lords of Trade and others.

Auteur anonyme - *Conduite des Français par rapport à la Nouvelle-Écosse*, Chez les Frères Vaillan, Londres 1755 (Exemplaire du Centre Acadien de l'Université Sainte-Anne. Cet ouvrage est une précieuse source de renseignements au sujet des rivalités entre l'Angleterre et la France, car l'auteur expose et refute les arguments des Anglais au sujet de leurs prétendus droits sur les colonies françaises d'Amérique.)

Emile Lauvrière - *La Tragédie d'un peuple - Histoire du peuple acadien de ses origines à nos jours*, Éditions Bossard, Paris, 1923.

Antoine Bernard - *Le Drame acadien depuis 1604*, Les Clercs de Saint-Viateur, Montréal, 1936.

Rameau de Saint-Père - *Une colonie féodale en Amérique*; La France aux Colonies, A Jouby, Librairie Editeur, Paris, 1859.

Beamish Murdoch - *A History of Nova Scotia or Acadia*, Vol. II, James Barnes, Printer, Halifax, N.S. 1865.

Public Archives of N.S. - *Minutes of His Majesty's Council at Annapolis Royal 1736-1749.*

Andrew Hill Clark - *Acadia, The Geography of Early Nova Scotia to 1760*, The University of Wisconsin Press, Madison, Wis. 1968.

Naomi Griffiths - *The Acadian Deportation: Deliberate Perfidy or Cruel Necessity?* Copp Clark Publishing Company, Toronto, 1969

The Acadians: Creation of A People, McGraw-Hill Ryerson, Toronto, 1973.

Dudley LeBlanc - *The True Story of the Acadians.* Dudley LeBlanc, 1937

The Acadian Miracle, Evangeline Publishing Company, Lafayette, La. 1966.

Placides Gaudet - *Le Grand Dérangement*, Ottawa, 1922.

CHAPTER X

An Examination of the Motives for the Expulsions

The Expulsion remains a turning point in the history of the Acadian ethnic group, and looms large among the events that determined the character of this people. An event of this magnitude, which changed the lives of so many for so long, cannot escape the scrutiny of the historians, who have all tried to logically explain or justify the Expulsion.

The most commonly used explanation is that it was a military necessity at the time, and it would appear from the letters of Governor Shirley of Massachusetts and Lawrence of Nova Scotia that such was the case, as the following quotations from their letters illustrate.

(June 18, 1746) The enemy will soon take Acadia, if we do not deport these dangerous settlers and replace them with British families.

(June 28, 1746) The province of N.S. will never be out of danger as long as the Acadians are tolerated there. If I had an army, I would lead it to Minas and Grand-Pré; I would break the dykes again; I would lay waste the whole country; I would drown this brood of vipers.

(July 19, 1747)....deporting the Acadians of Chignecto district (Beaubassin) somewhere in New England, dispersing them in all four provinces and replacing them by 2000 families from New England. Mr. Knowles (Commodore) with soldiers from New England could capture and deport all the inhabitants from Beaubassin. (Quoted from Shirley's letters)

Lawrence wrote in 1754:

No measures of security are adequate, so long as we shall not have absolutely eradicated the French from the Fort Beauséjour and all north of the Bay of Fundy. And Shirley answered: The longer we wait, the deeper the French will have entrenched themselves.

From these opinions expressed by persons in authority, it seems evident that the presence of the Acadians in N.S. was a menace to British power in the area. However, when the Acadians wanted to leave of their own free will they were prevented from doing so by the following governors: Vetch, Nicholson, Caulfield, Phillips, Mascarene, Doucett and even by Lawrence.

These assertions would also have more credibility had the attitude of the Acadians during the four invasions by Frenchmen in the 1740's not demonstrated that the Acadians as a group would not help their countrymen against the English.

Again MILITARY NECESSITY could hardly explain, and still less justify, the three deportations of the little communities in Southwestern Nova Scotia, or the persistent hunting down of stragglers after the main body of Acadians had been removed. It also fails to explain why the soldiers at Beauséjour, who had actually fought against the English, were allowed to remove themselves to Louisbourg, while the Acadians in the area were deported to the southernmost of the Thirteen Colonies. At Louisbourg, the French inhabitants and the soldiers were transported to France, while the Acadians found there were either deported to the Thirteen Colonies or to England. Using the argument of Military Expediency, the whole population of French Canada should have been deported in 1760 after the Conquest. But such was not the case.

Failure to take the Oath of Allegiance is another reason often invoked, yet the written opinions of Lawrence, Morris and Belcher demonstrate that the deportation would have been carried out regardless.

Lawrence said: "I will propose the Oath of Allegiance a last time. If they refuse we will have in that refusal a pretext for the Expulsion. If they accept, I will refuse them the oath by applying to them the decree which prohibits from taking the oath all persons who have once refused it. In both cases I shall deport them."

And Charles Morris, the Surveyor-General, made a report as to the best method of exiling the Acadians in which he said: "it makes no difference if they take the oath or not, they are at all adventures to be rooted out."

And Jonathan Belcher in his legal report says: "It is my duty to give my reasons why we should not allow the Acadians to take the oath and to tolerate them any longer in N.S."

Immediately after the capture of Quebec, two hundred Acadians who had sought refuge there applied to the authorities, for the purpose of taking the oath of allegiance and thereby obtaining permission to return to Acadia. After taking the oath, Judge Cramahe gave them signed certificates attesting that these people had taken the oath, and that consequently Murray had permitted them to return to their lands or to settle on the St. John River. They reached Fort Frederick toward the end of November and presented their certificates to Col. Arbuthnot, who commanded the post. He referred the matter to Lawrence, who ordered that they should be brought to Halifax to be exiled to the colonies.

The profit motive is often invoked as an overriding reason for the removal of the Acadians from the province especially by the French historians. The following is a quotation from Winslow's letters, dated June 14, 1755.

for among other consideration, the part of the country which they occupy is one of the best soils in the world, and in the event we might place some good British farmers on their homesteads.

It must also be remembered that the Acadians occupied the best lands of N.S. and in the opinion of Shirley, Belcher and Lawrence, constituted an unsurmountable obstacle to settlement of British subjects. Queen Anne's proclamation in 1713 had given them the right to sell their land, therefore even if they left the province and kept the titles to their land, this land would have to be bought, so this good land could not have been granted free to incoming British subjects. In order to disposess the Acadians of their lands they had to be condemned as rebels and exiled. Winslow expresses this opinion in the preceding quote and Belcher, in his judgment says: "Their refusal to take the oath precludes their right to hold property" and also: "Their continued presence in Nova Scotia.... would impede the progress of the settlement of the English colonists and prevent the realization of the projects which Great Britain had in mind when making considerable expenditures in that province."

Profits did accrue from the Expulsion, but not immediately and not to the persons mostly connected with it. The New England soldiers who carried out most of the Expulsion "either quitted the service or became dram sellers" said Lawrence. Lawrence, from all accounts, did not enrich himself (he got one fine stallion, sent to him by Monkton from the Acadians' animals). However some members of the council that decreed the Deportation, notably Mr. Saul, enriched himself from the sale of the Acadian cattle and hogs to the garrisons, and also from his commission on the hiring of the transports. The lands were left idle for five years or more before any settlers came. Not all of the vacant Acadian lands were taken then. Belcher and other members of the council, however, had granted themselves large tracts of land in Annapolis Valley and in Cumberland County. It must be pointed out that at the time of the Expulsion not all available land in N.S. had been taken, and enough land could have been granted to counterbalance the Acadian population by an influx of English Protestant settlers. (This was advocated by Shirley in his milder moments.)

The province itself did not profit from the Expulsion, as immediately prior to Lawrence's death in 1760, the citizens of Halifax petitioned the government of England to investigate Lawrence's administration, as the funds of the province had been wasted, and the goods of the Acadians had not been used to benefit the greatest number.

The Expulsion did not add to development of the province.

The areas once occupied by the Acadians have not proved to be the areas of greatest growth, which has taken place around Halifax and Sydney, where there were no Acadians in 1755.

While not one of the above motives is sufficient by itself to have set in motion the operation against the Acadians, a combination of the three, together with the whole situation in North America, provoked this drastic action.

It must be remembered that in 1755 the war for the mastery of the American continent had started and Lawrence, Belcher, and Shirley could not, or did not want to believe, that the Acadians would not take up arms with the French-Canadians and the French against the British occupation of Acadia. They felt that their positions and the territories under their command were in danger; it was not in their nature to take any chances in this matter. As it turned out the Expulsion made no difference in the outcome of the struggle, as the territory occupied by the Acadians remained outside the conflict throughout the war.

Furthermore, this action had been part of the British colonial policy "since 1658" as says Brebner in *New England Outpost*, p. 201.

In 1720, the Colonial Office had written to Governor Philipps. "They (the Acadians) must be transported to some place where mingling with our subjects, they will soon lose their language, their religion, and the remembrance of the past." Quoted from Edouard Richard, *Acadia*, Montreal 1895, Vol. 1, p. 124.

One must also remember that France was still the most powerful nation on the European continent, so the fear of France played its part in the decision to remove the Acadians. In the ten years prior to the Deportation, France had launched four attacks against Acadia. Even though the great majority of Acadians had remained neutral, some had given aid to the invaders. All this inspired an atmosphere of hysterical fear compounded by hatred of everything French and / or Catholic. This fear of France remained even after French power was destroyed in America. A surprise raid by France against St. John's, Newfoundland, in 1762, resulted in all the Acadians who were permitted to work in N.S., (in the Valley and around Halifax), to be rounded up and with those held in Halifax and deported once more to Boston. However Massachusetts refused to accept them and shipped them back to Halifax. Even after 1763, Acadians did not have permission to settle in Cape Breton, as it was feared that France would use those Acadians on St. Pierre and Miquelon, to plot with those on Cape Breton, to retain some influence or some power in the Gulf.

The problem and the fear of the Indians was a factor in decreeing the Expulsion.

The correspondence of Lawrence, Belcher and Shirley indicate their firm belief that, with the Acadians totally removed from the whole area of the present Maritime Provinces, the Indians would make peace with the English, but that while even a few Acadians remained with them, the Indians would deal with the French and prey on the English settlements.

It must also be remembered that dislike of the Acadians was fanned by the desire of vengeance on the part of the Anglo-Americans who had been subjected to savage raids by the Indians, aided by the French from Canada, and the "captains of the savages"* of Acadia. The French-Canadians and the Indians were often beyond their grasp but the vengeance could be easily directed against the defenceless Acadians. The Acadians were also convenient scapegoats for the desire of vengeance by the New England merchants and fishermen, for their losses at the

* The "captains of the savages", an expression used by Rameau de Saint-Pierre, in describing the role of the so-called seigneurs, such as the d'Amours brothers, La Mothe Cadillac, Solanges and Saint-Castin who were granted large tracts of land along the Saint John River and in Maine not so much to develop agricultural communities but to trade with the Indians and keep these on friendly terms with the French.

hands of French privateers, who had operated from Port-Royal and now were operating from Louisbourg.

The English settlers of New England and those around Halifax also feared an uprising by the Acadians and Indians. In fact a number of settlers in the Halifax area had their throats slashed by Indians, friends of the Acadians.

Another motive which has not been recalled too often, but appears in some of the correspondence of Lawrence, Winslow, and Shirley was the desire on the part of the authorities to settle Nova Scotia with settlers from New England.

SOURCE OF INFORMATION

Same as for Chapter IX

CHAPTER XI

The Acadians Maintain Their Ethnic Identity

Shirley and Lawrence had seen the Deportation as the extermination of the Acadians as a people, because they would be absorbed by the population of the Thirteen Colonies and lose their language, religion and memories of the past.

A number of circumstances and the character of the victims prevented this disappearance, and instead led to a strengthening of the ethnic bond.

Among these was the fact that the Acadians were never permitted to become a part of the society into which they were thrust. The treatment they received in all the colonies helped to keep them together, and removed all desire to remain and integrate in the Anglo-Protestant society of the Thirteen Colonies. The reception they received on their return to their old holdings in Nova Scotia also prevented their mixing with the New England settlers, who were now occupying their lands.

The conditions of the Expulsion itself proved to be a rallying point, a common experience that linked them all together, and etched in their minds the fact that they were distinct from any other ethnic group.

Necker, the minister of Louis XVI, said of those who were in France that they formed the "core of a nation".

The patterns of resettlement of Acadians, whether in Atlantic Canada, Quebec, France or Louisiana, contributed in no small measure in keeping intact their cultural identity. Either by design of the authorities, or by choice of the settlers themselves, the Acadians were granted land outside the main concentrations of the majority groups of the countries in which they settled.

In Nova Scotia they obtained land along Saint Mary's Bay, on points of land in Yarmouth County, on Ile Madame, and on the north shore of Inverness County.

In France they were assigned land on an island off the Coast of Britany, and in a depopulated area of Poitou. Those who went to the French islands of Saint Pierre and Miquelon chose the latter rather than the more populated Saint Pierre, and in

Louisiana they were given land in the bayou country outside the areas already settled by the Creoles. They therefore remained "Cajuns" with a totally different way of life and set of values from the first settlers of this colony who spoke a similar language and practiced the same faith.

The *family structure of the Acadians* was a strong contributing factor to the maintenance of the ethnic identity under these most adverse conditions.

The Acadians had developed a closely knit family pattern in their pioneer settlement. This continued wherever they went during and after the period of the Expulsion. They continued to marry among themselves rather than choose mates from other ethnic groups with whom they were in contact, even in Quebec and in France, although not to the same extent as in Atlantic Canada.

The separation of families during that period was carried out: "in the hope that in time, their manners, language and predilections would be changed, and even the recollection of their origin lost", as Haliburton so aptly puts it. However that very separation had the opposite result.

It prevented them from wanting to take roots anywhere until they had exhausted all means of reuniting their families. Had families been removed as units to one locality in the Thirteen Colonies and given land there, they might have been more inclined to remain. As it was done, they left the colonies as soon as they could, to rejoin other members of their group. This search for the missing members of the family was a predominant concern of the group, and family ties were often the deciding factor in the choice of a place to resettle. Practically all the families that settled in Clare had close ties and the few unrelated families soon left the area to settle elsewhere with other members of their family, such was the case of Joseph Gravois, Joseph Bonnevie, Jean Belonie LeBlanc and Amable Richard.

Religion

As mentioned before one of the most outstanding traits of the Acadian was his deep faith in the Catholic religion, which he carried throughout the long years of his exile. This religious faith kept him apart from his neighbors whether he was in England, in the Thirteen Colonies (except Maryland;) and after 1760, in Nova Scotia.

It prevented his mixing with non-Catholic groups, because these groups were as adverse to intermarriage with Catholics as the Acadians were to mixing with non-Catholics. The Catholic faith had taught the Acadians patience and perseverance, and prevented them from saying during this difficult period: "What's the use? Let's abandon our religion and language and join the majority." Instead of accepting the easy way out, they kept their faith for it was to them a source of strength. Their Catholicism was all the more dear to them because they felt persecuted because of it.

Pierre Belliveau, in *French Neutrals in Massachusetts*, says that the more the Puritans tried to show the Acadians the error of their religious beliefs, the more firmly the Acadians rejected attempts to convert them. They feared their children being taken away from them to be converted to protestantism.

So, in spite of all difficulties, the Acadians still remained as a distinct group after peace was restored between England and France. Furthermore they wished to remain as a group and knew that they could not do so if they remained scattered as they were. As a result they set out to find new homes where they hoped to continue a way of life which had become vital to them. This led to a pattern of resettlement peculiar to them which will be the subject of the next chapter.

CHAPTER XII

Acadian Resettlements after the Expulsion

We have already seen that the Acadians were forced to "migrate" to the Thirteen Colonies and to England in 1755, while those who escaped this forced migration chose to make their way to Quebec via Chaleur Bay or the Saint John River.

From 1755 to 1763 there were other forced migrations such as the 3500 Acadians who were repatriated from Isle Saint-Jean and Isle Royale to France.

But after 1763 these forced migrations ceased, and the Acadians could have remained where they were. Most of them chose to set out on their travels again, in spite of the many hardships that these incurred, because the alternative of staying where they were, proved far less attractive.

Reasons for leaving the areas in which they lived in 1760-64:

We have already seen that the Acadians were treated as undesirable aliens in all the Thirteen Colonies except Maryland. Excepting Maryland, the Colonies would not grant land or allow them to own property, unless they forsook their religion and took an absolute oath of allegiance. Some colonies would not even give them this opportunity, but Massachusetts did offer them land. In Georgia and in North and South Carolina, they had to work with the slaves under the same conditions. In New York they remained at best bonded servants.

In the southern states, the physical conditions, climate and work in the tobacco and cotton fields under the same conditions as the negro slaves made living almost impossible for the Acadians who had been free, and used to a northern climate.

A large group left Halifax in 1764 to go to San Domingo, because they would not take the oath of allegiance. There the political climate was better, but the physical climate unbearable, so in 1765 they moved on to Louisiana.

In France also, the Acadians did not find the political climate to their liking. They especially resented the status of peasants bound to the soil under the feudal system. They preferred taking jobs in town and having someone else work the land allotted to them. They were not afraid to tell officials that certain lands allotted for farming were not suitable. Finally many of them left for Louisiana, so that by the end of 1785 only about 1600 Acadians were left in France.

The desire to unite the extended family was a great influence in causing the Acadians to move from one place to another, in the hope of finding another member of their dispersed family. Whenever they heard of members of their family settled in a certain region, they were drawn to that locality as by a magnet. It seems that there were various avenues of communication to enable them to unite, in spite of their illiteracy and the lack of means of communication in those days.

The hope of settling on their own homesteads drew many back to Nova Scotia and southeastern New Brunswick. To fulfill this dream many trekked from Georgia, the Carolinas and Massachusetts and sailed from England and France in ships bound for old Acadie. Possibly many more would have come back had there been more possibility of regaining title to their land.

Acadian settlements in the Maritime Provinces (Nova Scotia, Prince Edward Island and New Brunswick)

At the end of the hostilities in 1763 there were approximately 1,019 Acadians* in Nova Scotia which then comprised all three present Maritime Provinces. The British government had

* Based on a list of Acadians wanting to go to a French territory found in a letter from "Beausoleil" Broussard, presented to the Council at Halifax, August 18, 1763. Public Archives of Canada

instructed the colonial authorities that it was no longer a good policy to deport the Acadians. They could remain in the colony and receive land, provided they took the oath of allegiance.

Some of them preferred to leave rather than to take the hated oath. A group of 164 former detainees at Halifax, led by Joseph "Beausoleil" Broussard, chartered a boat and sailed for the French West Indian Island of San Domingo. The tropical climate proved disastrous to them and many died soon after arriving. The survivors, still led by 'Beausoleil" Broussard then sailed to Louisiana where they finally settled around the Poste des Attakapas, in the southwestern part of the colony sometime prior to April 4, 1765. On that date, Joseph Broussard signed a contract with Antoine Bernard d'Hauterive, who agreed to supply livestock to the Acadians. Among the other Acadians who signed the contract were Pierre Arcenaud, Alexandre, Jean-Baptiste and Victor Broussard, Jean Dugas, Joseph Guillebeau and Olivier Thibodeau. From these settlers and others who joined them from Nova Scotia, the West Indies and Maryland have grown the parishes of Saint Martin, Lafayette, Iberia, Vermilion and Saint Mary.

Others, who left Halifax and vicinity for the same reason as Joseph Broussard and his companions, went to the French Islands of Saint-Pierre and Miquelon. They left in small groups at different times, so that by 1767 there were 551* Acadians on these Islands, mostly on Miquelon where they could continue their self-sufficient economy by farming and fishing.

Many among the detainees at Halifax knew that there had been a small French settlement not far from Halifax, established just prior to the Expulsion by Lapierre. Many made their way to this place and eventually settled there, among others Lapierres, Petitpas, Bellefontaines, LeBlancs.This is now Chezzetcook.

* Census taken by Dangeac, May 15, 1767.

The problem of settling the others who were willing to take the oath of allegiance still remained. Governor Wilmot and his council were torn between compliance with the advice to grant lands to the Acadians, and their deep distrust of the French. Finally in 1764, they consented to grant lots of land to Acadian families, provided that they took the oath of allegiance. The lots would be allocated on the basis of 40 acres to the head of the family and 10 acres for each additional member. Ten of these lots were to be in Wilmot Township, 10 in Lunenburg Township, 30 in Halifax Township, 10 in Horton, 10 in Annapolis, and so forth. This system would isolate the Acadian communities and eventually assimilate them in the surrounding Anglo-Saxon community. Furthermore these lots would be inland, so as to prevent easy communication between these former French Neutrals and the French on Saint-Pierre and Miquelon.

This scheme never materialized. Instead many Acadians took matters into their own hands. Many who had been living on Ile Madame before the Expulsion returned there, even without obtaining permission from the authorities. This is evident from a letter from Charles Morris to the council at Halifax in 1764, who said that there were 14 Acadian families living there then. The letter goes on to express concern over the presence of so many Acadians in close proximity to their compatriots on the French Islands of St-Pierre and Miquelon, who could join together and recapture Cape Breton Island!

In spite of this supposed threat, the government did not take any effective measures to stop the growth of the settlements in southwestern Cape Breton, so that by 1774 there were 502 Acadians settled there. Many of these were really returning to their former homes, as many of the family names on Isle Madame today were in the census of Isle Madame and Isle Royale compiled by de la Rocque in 1752.

Meanwhile, in 1767, another group of 42 Acadian heads of families petitioned for land, and were granted large acreages in the Cocagne and Shediac areas. From these original settlers and others who joined them from the Massachusetts grew the Acadian villages and towns of southeastern New Brunswick such as Cocagne, Bouctouche, Richibouctou.

The so-called "Caravan from Massachusetts" was made up of some 800 Acadian men, women, and children who assembled at Salem in 1766 and set out on foot to seek their old homes in their beloved Acadie. They kept no record of how many died along the way, but the mortality rate must have been fairly high, from the stories handed down orally from generation to generation.

When the group arrived at Saint Anne's on the Saint John River, they found some Acadian families already settled there. A number of families from the "caravan" felt they had travelled enough, and decided to stay there in the area of what was to become Fredericton. However, they soon were advised that very few of them would be allowed to remain by an Order in Council, October 5, 1767.

Some of the group decided to move on to the region of Memramcook, where they found some compatriots who had escaped the Deportation, and had resettled on lands that they had occupied before 1755. Most of the families in the "caravan" stopped here, and if the expression "pitched their tent" would be inappropriate it would be correct to say they erected their squared log cabins on the hills overlooking the Memramcook valley.

Not all of them stopped there, however. Some felt the pull of the magnets that were Piziquid, Grand-Pré and Port Royal and continued their trek buoyed by the hope of finding again their beloved homes, remnants of their herds of cattle, their aboiteaux, their orchards and for a few, their small hoards of coins that they had cached during the summer of 1755. (It is a fact that a number of these caches of French coins were found by the Planters who occupied these lands after 1760).

Alas! these hopes were dashed for all their lands were being farmed by the New England Planters, who looked askance at these ghosts from the past who might cause them trouble. The

Acadians felt less than welcomed in their old homes and decided to move on once more. From their temporary quarters at Windsor they petitioned the Governor for a priest from Quebec, and a surveyor to survey land they begged to have. Governor Michael Franklin acceded to both their demands. Father Charles Bailly de Messein came as missionary to the Indians and to the Acadians, and by a Warrant of Survey, dated July 1, 1768, the governor authorized John Morrison, Deputy Surveyor, to survey the future township of Clare, extending from the Sissiboo River to Cape Saint Mary. It was to be divided into lots on the basis of 80 acres for the head of a family and 20 acres for each other member of the family.

The first settler to take advantage of the land granted in the township of Clare was Joseph Dugas, who settled with his wife and daughter at Anse des LeBlanc, in the parish of Saint Bernard in September 1768. His son Joseph was born 20 days after their arrival.

Other settlers followed in the spring of 1769 and following years. These first received Licenses of Occupation, before receiving the official grant in 1775. It is from these grantees of 1775 that most of the (9,000) Acadians in Digby County descend.

Meanwhile, some Acadian families from the Cape Sable area who had been deported to Massachusetts returned by their own ship in 1766. Naturally, they were attracted to their former lands but these were already occupied by settlers from New England.

The minutes of the Council at Halifax reveal that on October 5, 1767, 18 Acadian families applied for land on which to settle. They were advised that on taking the oath of allegiance, they would be assigned lands in the neighbourhood of Barrington and Yarmouth. They chose both sides of Pubnico Harbour and settled with "Licenses of Occupation". In November 1771, 5700 acres were granted to Joseph, Paul, Benoni d'Entremont, Abel Duon, Jacques and Ange Amirault and Charles Belliveau, Philip

Brown, Walter Larkin, Benjamin Sealy, Petitiah Goodwin and others. All of these received additional grants later on the eastern side of Pubnico Harbour.

Even before the arrival of these settlers in the Pubnico area, Joseph Moulaison had settled on Surette's Island in 1764, on land given to him by Ronald McKinnon who had obtained previously a large grant comprising the points and inlets on the southern tip of Yarmouth County. Jacques Amirault, Jr. settled on part of this grant and founded the village of Amirault's Hill.

Apart from the land that was granted in 1771 to Benoni d'Entremont and 17 others at Pubnico, all the rest of the present district of Argyle had been granted, either to immigrants from New England or in large tracts to Ronald McKinnon, Ebenezer Moulton and the Reverend John Breynton. As these three could not possibly fulfill all the obligations of the grants within the specified time limit, they were willing to sell part or all of their holdings at a minimal price to willing settlers, or at least have settlers on them.

This appealed to many Acadians eagerly looking for land. To take advantage of these offers, Eustache Corporon, Pierre Robicheau, Jean Doucette and Pierre Inard came to Tusket Wedge (Wedgeport) in 1767. In 1773 they bought 1500 acres from Ebenezer Moulton. Other families joined them after the purchase.

The area of Sainte-Anne-du-Ruisseau and Belleville was settled, from 1767 on, by seven families who bought part of the grant of Rev. John Breynton. Most of the Acadians living in the parish of Sainte-Anne-du-Ruisseau are descendants of these seven families.

We have already mentioned that a number of families had settled without permission around Saint-Anne on the Saint John River. When the Loyalists arrived after the American Revolution, they were granted lands occupied by the Acadians, who were told to leave on short notice but that they could apply and receive grants of land in the Madawaska region in the upper reaches of the Saint John River. Consequently Louis Mercure applied for a grant for himself and 21 others and Jean-Baptiste Cyr applied for himself and his nine sons. The petitions were granted and in 1785, 16 Acadian families settled on both sides of the Saint John River, in the present counties of Victoria and Madawaska counties in New Brunswick, and Aroostook County in Maine.

All the displaced persons of Sainte-Anne did not stop in the Madawaska territory, but continued to the shores of Chaleur Bay where many of their relatives had already taken root.

Some of them had taken refuge there during the time of the Expulsion, and having escaped capture in spite of a number of raids, had remained in the area throughout the war years.

In speaking of the way of life of the Acadians we mentioned that 30 families, (according to Holland's report), had remained on Prince Edward Island. It is from these 30 families that descend most of the 15,000 Acadians now living in Prince Edward Island. Although they are found throughout the Island, the largest concentrations are in the County of Prince, and around Rustico in the County of Queens.

Life was not always easy for them under the regime of the absentee landlords. These people found it particularly frustrating to work on land that had been theirs in the past, and for which they now had to pay rent and could never hope to own. Such conditions of tenure drove many to seek land elsewhere. Some crossed over to Kent County in New Brunswick, and in 1785-86, 18 families went to a fine harbour on the coast of Cape Breton, a place now called Chéticamp.

From the 18 families grew the villages of Chéticamp, Saint-Joseph-du-Moine, Grand Etang, Petit Etang, Belle Marche, le Plateau. Some 6,645 people of Acadian descent live there today, while many other descendants of these families form a good proportion of the population of the Sydney, Glace Bay, New Waterford area.

Thus by 1785, the displaced Acadians were resettled in

widely separated areas of the former province of Nova Scotia, now divided into three provinces and also formed the core of the population of the Magdalen Islands.

They had also settled in the province of Quebec, and in France and its possessions, as we shall explain.

Acadian settlements in Quebec

The Acadians recovered in Quebec some of the territory they had lost in Acadia.

It was only in 1766 that the British government, free from the French menace now that all of Canada was in its possession, decided that allowing the Acadians to settle in Quebec would be an asset rather than a hindrance. Consequently the governments of the Thirteen Colonies granted permission to the Acadians to leave these colonies and to seek lands elsewhere.

However they were still not welcomed in Nova Scotia. Governor Wilmot still feared that their return would endanger the safety of the province. It would have been so easy for them to take passage on vessels leaving the northeastern ports for Halifax and Yarmouth, but the masters of the vessels were instructed not to take them aboard. With the sea route partially blocked to them, there remained the land route, which required little money but plenty of hardships. Most of them took this route.

One group of about 800 took the coast route which led them back to Acadia as we have already seen.

Others took the Hudson-Mohawk-Lake Champlain route - these were the settlers of the Acadias of the Montreal and the Three Rivers regions. Sieur Péan de Chamblay in a letter to Lévis, 1758, says:

"The Acadians escaped from Boston three weeks ago and are now at St-Jean".

Moreau says:

"Badly treated by the Puritans of New England, they succeeded in escaping from Salem. Guided by Indians they followed the Mohawk Trail. It was not too difficult to reach Lake Champlain, then to follow the Richelieu to Montreal. Some stopped at a place called Petite Cadie (L'Acadie), and others reached the St. Lawrence where they settled at St-Jacques de l'Achigan. The best known of these settlers were Lanoue, Hébert, Cyr, Godin, Babin, Granger, Bourgeois".

The Intendant Bigot wrote on Feb. 15, 1758:

"More than 1500 Acadians came to Quebec of whom 400 died from smallpox. But some had arrived before this, some by water but others have come by land. 500 came from the English colonies by way of Lake Champlain and have stopped south of Montreal".

From documents of the period it appears that most of the Acadians chose the site of L'Acadie for their home and then made arrangements to stay there with the "seigneurs" of the area. The area comprised three seigneuries - Longeuil, the Jesuit seigneury of La Prairie, and the seigneury de Lery. The government of Quebec asked the seigneurs to establish the Acadians on their lands "on the best possible conditions". Nothing shows what these best possible conditions were, but they do not appear to have been very different from those made to anyone else. Some Acadians, especially those who came between 1755 and 1768, did take land as squatters: they were either ignored or tolerated but never evicted, and some bought their land with paper money that they had received for goods sold to the British before 1755, and which was redeemable now that Britain was in possession of New France.

The region of Acadie south of Montreal prospered. In fact it is a very fertile area and even to-day is the leading supplier of agricultural products to Montreal. It has remained a rural area, characteristic of the Acadians, and has spread out to form the neighbouring parishes of St-Remi, Napierville, St-Luc, St-Jean, St-Jacques, St-Blaise.

The church of Acadie, constructed in 1801, has been a provincial historical monument since 1957.

Family names found in this area are: Arsenault, Arpin, Beliveau, Boudreau, Gaudet, Landry, LeBlanc, Marin, Morin, Poirier, Richard, Robichaud, Theriault, Thibodeau, Trahan.

St-Jacques de l'Achigan

The first real welcome extended to the Acadians in Quebec was by the Sulpician Fathers who had a large tract of land, on the north side of the St. Lawrence River, on a river known as l'Achigan. They received thirteen families in 1766, and forty more in 1767. Most of these came from Connecticut. They prospered for they paid no rent before 1779, and the Sulpician Order built them a flour mill and a saw mill.

From the original village of St-Jacques de l'Achigan the inhabitants spread out to found parishes at St-Alexis, St-Liguori, Rawdon, Ste-Julienne, Crabtree, Ste-Marie, Salome, Epithanie. The total area became for them the Acadian centre of Québec.

The Acadie of the Quebec Region

After the fall of Beauséjour in 1755, a large number of Acadians managed to escape being captured by Monckton's soldiers; and even after their buildings and crops were destroyed, they refused to give themselves up. They gathered together at Miramichi where their situation was desperate, for they had no food nor shelter.

The government at Quebec did send them supplies when advised of their predicament, and the ships which took supplies to them arrived back at Quebec laden with refugees in miserable condition. They received little help there, since there was a food shortage among the population, and many died from malnutrition and other diseases. Those remaining were exploited to the limit by two scoundrels, Duchenoux and Péan, who cut their already meagre rations, and allowed them only one-half to two-thirds of the value of their paper money which they had received for supplies delivered in the preceding years to Louisbourg and Beauséjour.

Péan and his wife, who had an unoccupied seigneury near Quebec, encouraged Acadians to settle on these lands. It was a gesture planned to fill their own pockets, for the government was now helping these Acadians who were settling on French territory, and the Péans succeeded in channelling to their own coffers all the subsidies destined for the Acadian settlers. They were helped in their exploitation by Duchenoux, who was a protégé of the Intendant Bigot. Bigot and Péan returned to France and had to answer to their dealings before the French Court but Duchenoux remained in Canada and in 1766 bought Péan's seigneury. He then befriended the English governor and was able not only to enjoy his ill-gotten gains, but to turn his seigneury into one of the most profitable in Quebec, thanks to the hard working Acadians. He also attracted to his seigneury the Acadians who came to Quebec after 1766, and enlarged his holdings by acquiring the seigneuries of de la Durantaye, Beaumont, Livaudière.

As for the number of the original Acadian settlers in the Acadie of Quebec, we find: 20 families in 1756, 23 more in 1757, 5 more in 1758. Many more came after 1766, but some left and some died, so that by 1770 there were 60 families. During the American Revolution many left the area - only 55 families were reported in 1780, but in 1825, there were 507 families and since then the increase in families and population has been rapid.

Becancour

The Acadians arrived in this area in three groups. The first group came with the approximately 2000 Acadians who came to Quebec after the fall of Beauséjour. This group had L'Abbé LeGuerne as parish priest. He assembled them first in the area of Miramichi (in New Brunswick), but when he was appointed parish priest at St-François on the Island of Orleans, he pleaded the cause of the Acadians before the government of Québec, which sent ships to bring them to Québec. Some of them remained behind, but many others kept on up the St. Lawrence to Becancour.

A second group came from the St. John River area. These followed the St. John River to the Temiscouta and arrived at Cacouna on the St. Lawrence, whence they proceeded to Quebec. Here sickness and famine were prevalent, so they continued on to the Three Rivers area where they found land available, and better living conditions.

The third group was comprised of Acadians who came from the New England States after 1766-67. This third group seemed to have been attracted to the area because some of their relatives were already established there. Some, too, were helped to the region by the Abanaki Indians, who had a settlement and mission near the Becancour region.

Moreover the territory of Becancour - Godefroy had large areas of unsettled land and large tracts of forest with plenty of game, providing the settlers with an immediate and plentiful food supply. It seems that at first they considered this region as a temporary refuge, hoping to return to their native Acadie as soon as possible. Only after this hope faded did they decide to make the areas of Becancour - Batiscan another second Acadie.

The Acadians in France, their origin and resettlement

Some 1200 Acadians from the Beauséjour area were destined for Virginia, but were refused admission to that colony, and shipped to England where they were held as prisoners of war until 1763. The death rate on the voyage to England and in England itself was very high, for by 1763, there were only 741 left. These all chose to go to France and were landed at Morlaix in Britany.

Another group came from the Cape Sable area. They had first been kept as prisoners in Halifax, and then sent to England and then to France. These were landed at Cherbourg. There is no explanation why this British ship landed its passengers at Cherbourg, but from the parish records of Cherbourg, these Acadians from the Cape Sable area were there in 1758, 1759 or 1760. The third group, and by far the largest, comprised the

Acadians repatriated from Isle Saint-Jean (Prince Edward Island) and Louisbourg in the Fall of 1758 and the Spring of 1759. 2,200 were thus landed in France at this time. We know from the archives of the Ministry of the Colonies that 138 Acadians from Boulogne, of whom 62 were from Acadia, 52 from Louisbourg and 26 from Isle St-Jean, were sent to Guyana in 1764 and were brought back to France in 1765.

We know that 78 families were established on the Island of Belle-Isle-en-Mer, and it has remained the most lasting of the Acadian establishments in France. Belle-Isle was chosen because of the fact that it had unoccupied land available for the destitute Acadians. The reason for this unoccupied land was due to the fact that during the Seven Years War, in 1761, Belle-Isle-en-Mer had been occupied by England and some of the inhabitants driven out. In 1763 it was ceded back to France. The Acadians, accustomed to combining fishing and farming, seemed adapted to life on Belle-Isle. Three Acadians came to inspect the Island and reported favourably to their compatriots. These three were from the Minas Basin area, and their names were: Honoré LeBlanc, Joseph-Simon Granger and Joseph Trahan. The governments of France and Britany made arrangements to settle 78 families on the island, but the response was not enthusiastic. At first only 25 families accepted the offer. The Acadians were in no hurry to leave their free lodgings and subsidies at Morlaix. It took l'Abbé LeLoutre, who had just been released from prison on Jersey Island, to convince 77 families from Morlaix to settle on Belle-Isle. Another family from Boulogne-sur-mer joined them.

However, French government machinery in those days was ponderous and slow moving. It was only in November 1765 that 78 families comprising some 400 persons arrived on the Island. The conditions were fairly generous. They were to receive three months ration, free tobacco, all required tools, a boat, payment of the rent they had to pay in Morlaix from the time they accepted the offer. Each family was to receive 20 journaux of land, 10 of meadow and two of pasture (a journal of land was the area of land that could be plowed by a man and a team of oxen in a day), plus a barn, a pair of oxen, a cow, a horse, a cart, a plow, iron and coal for repairing their farm implements, and also some money to buy sheep.

However the settlement was not a success. No one received the promised 37 "journaux" of land. The poor soil and dry climate produced only meagre crops that discouraged these former farmers of Acadia. Many left between 1772 and 1775. Of the original families - LeBlanc, Granger, Melanson, Richard, Trahan, Pitre, Aucoin, Boudreau, Hébert, Duon, Terriot, Babin, Douaron, Landry, Thibaudault, Goutrot, Poirier, Doucet, there are still some Grangers, Gouthros, Melansons and Duons living there now. The island had a maximum population of about 10,000 at the turn of the century but it has fallen to about 5400 now. The descendants of the Acadian settlers of 1765 are still proud of their Acadian ancestry and celebrated their bicentennial in 1965, when they welcomed a group of Acadians from Canada.

Another plan was to settle 1500 Acadians in the Poitou region, a plan which matured in 1772, at which time there were about 2563 Acadians in France. Some 1500 answered the invitation to take land there but the settlement was a failure, and by 1775 most of the Acadians were back in the towns they had left, with most of them converging on Nantes. From there they emigrated back to Acadia or to Louisiana, so that by 1785 most of them had left France. In that year, 1629 Acadians left Nantes for New Orleans, the largest single group to leave for Louisiana.

However all traces of their settlement in Poitou were not erased. Twenty-five families remained. By 1789 they had 58 houses, all built by the state. In 1793, the head of each Acadian family received one, two, three, or even five grants of land. This area of Poitou is still known as the *Acadian Line,* and strangely enough, in this region new houses are constructed today, the farms are well-kept and expanded, while all around the countryside the French villages are abandoned and farms are neglected. Some Acadian names found in this area are: Daigle,

Boudrot, Landry, Melançon, Brault, Gautreau, Theriot, Doucet, Bunel, Hébert.

Thus by the end of the seventeenth century the Acadians were dispersed, by choice and circumstance, from Quebec to Louisiana in America and in many isolated pockets in France, while still maintaining a strong foothold in their native Acadie. In spite of the dispersal, the culture which grew during their 150 years in Old Acadia survived in the areas where they now live.

CHAPTER XIII

The Acadians Today

People of Acadian descent number some 240,000 in New Brunswick or about 37% of the population of that province. They are concentrated in the counties of Madawaska, Victoria, Restigouche, Gloucester and Kent, where they form the majority of the population. They are numerous in the counties of Northumberland, Westmorland and Saint John, but they are also found in smaller numbers in the other counties of the province.

In Nova Scotia, the Acadians numbered approximately 84,000 according to the last census, or about 10% of the total population, a percentage which has remained fairly constant for the last one hundred years. In Nova Scotia the people of Acadian descent are found mostly in the counties of Yarmouth, Digby, Inverness, Richmond, Halifax, and Antigonish. At present they do not have a majority in any of these counties.

In Prince Edward Island, the Acadians account for 14% of the population of Prince County, concentrated in the Evangeline District, and a small percentage of the population of Kings and Queens counties.

In Atlantic Canada, outside of the Maritimes, Acadians form the largest percentage of the population of the Magdalen Islands, where they number some 10,000 out of a population of 12,500. There is also an Acadian community around Saint Georges' Bay on the West coast of Newfoundland.

The economy

The fishery and related industries are the mainstay of the Acadian communities of all Atlantic Canada. Lobster fishing is the dominant fishery in all coastal Acadian communities, but fishing for other species, such as scallop, crab, herring and cod, is also very important and lucrative.

But Acadians have branched out in all the different trades and professions. To ply these trades,and exercise their professions, as doctors, lawyers, dentists, engineers, accountants, architects, and so forth, they had to migrate to the cities and towns, which accounts for a large out-migration from all the

Acadian villages to the urban areas not only of the Maritimes but of Quebec, Ontario, the West, and the United States. Even in the Acadian communities you can now find most of the trades and professions; in fact 63% of the work force in these communities is employed in the service sector of the economy.

Although the annual income of the people in the twelve counties of the Maritimes, where the Acadians form at least 20% of the population, is 9% less than for the Maritimes as a whole, this does not indicate a lower standard of living. The vast majority of these people own their homes and in a rural setting they can provide for themselves most of the necessities of life by practicing the self-sufficient type of economy of former days.

The Church and the community

The one and only church, usually on a hill dominating the village, is indicative of the role the Church played among these people. For a long time it was the rallying point of the community and the religious and social life of the rural Acadians revolved around it. It was in the forefront for the preservation of the cultural identity of the Acadians. It also promoted religious parish schools, convents and colleges and sponsored the parish credit unions and co-operatives.

Since the 1960's the Church has largely abandoned its dominant role in non-religious affairs in the community, and limits its activities to strictly religious functions. Although these functions are not as well attended as in the past, when 99% of the parish participated, the Acadians in general remain attached to the Catholic faith.

The family

Most villages in the Maritimes were settled by closely related families. In Belliveau Cove, Nova Scotia, a survey done in 1952, revealed that out of 296 persons in the village, 281 were related by blood or marriage to one of the four founding families and 31 related to two of these families. In West Pubnico, there were in the 1985 telephone directory 337 d'Entremont families, 118 d'Eons, 39 Amirault out of total of 606 subscribers. These closely related families account for a very homogeneous community, which acts as one large family and exerts great pressure on its individual members to behave in the best interest of the group. If any family suffers a misfortune all the related families come to its aid.

As in all pioneer communities, the Acadian pioneer family tended to have a large number of children. In northern New Brunswick ten to eighteen per family were not uncommon, and the five counties in which the Acadians were the large majority the birthrate was by far the highest in the Maritimes.

In Nova Scotia and Prince Edward Island the counties which have the most Acadians do not show a higher birthrate than the other counties, which would indicate that the Acadian families in these provinces were not larger than those of the other ethnic groups. At the present time the Acadian families follow the general trend of two or three children per family.

The Acadian family had a tendency to be very stable, as separations were discouraged by the community and divorces were not permitted in the Catholic Church to which they all belonged. Now, however, separations and divorces are as common among Acadians as they are in all other ethnic groups.

Education

There were no schools in the Acadian regions of the Maritimes before 1800, partly because a law of the Province of Nova Scotia, passed in 1766, forbade a Catholic to teach. Although rescinded twenty years later, the effects of it were felt for years afterwards, for no teachers had been formed among the Catholic Acadians.

The first teachers in the Acadian districts appeared in Nova Scotia in 1794, and the first improvised school was opened in Father Sigogne's glebe house in 1800. Following these examples itinerant teachers began to teach in the homes of the parents who wanted to have their children educated and priests opened their glebes for the Christian education of their young parishioners.

The Acadian sections of Nova Scotia had their schools where French was taught as a first language, from the 1830's to 1864 when the Free School Act was passed establishing unilingual English public schools. New Brunswick passed a similar law in 1871 and Prince Edward Island did the same in 1877.

Since that time the Acadian communities have waged a campaign for a school curriculum, based on the needs and aspirations of the French-speaking population of the Maritimes. The Official Languages Act of the Federal government, and the fact that New Brunswick is officially bilingual, aided the struggle of Acadian educators for a greater use of French in the curriculum.

At the present time New Brunswick has a separate school system for the Acadian regions, supervised by a deputy-minister of education. In these sections French is taught as the first language, and the language of instruction is French for all subjects, except English, from primary to twelve. The technical and trade schools in the Acadian sections also receive their instruction in French.

In Nova Scotia, Bill 65 passed in 1981, officially recognizes Acadian Schools in which all subjects except English is taught in French in the first six grades. In Junior High grades there is a minimum of ten courses taught in French, and in Senior High a minimum of eight courses are taught in French. It is, however, possible for a student to take all his or her courses in French, except English.

In Prince Edward Island the Acadian section of Prince County, the Evangeline section, a similar programme is implemented.

The first Acadian institution of higher learning was Saint Joseph University in Memramcook, New Brunswick, founded in 1864. The next was College Saint Louis fcunded in 1874. After a promising beginning it had to close ten years later under pressure from the Bishop of Chatham, Mgr. Rogers. The Eudist Fathers founded Saint Anne's College at Church Point in 1890, and the Sacred Heart College at Caraquet in 1899. After the building at Caraquet burned, the Eudists transferred the institution to Bathurst. In 1946 the Eudist Fathers opened the College Saint-Louis in Edmunston, N.-B. Four colleges were later opened for girls in New Brunswick: College Maillet at Saint Basile, College Jesus-Marie at Shippegan, College Assumpta at Bathurst and College Notre-Dame at Moncton.

Since 1972 all these French colleges in New Brunswick amalgamated into one French institution of higher learning supported by the province, the University of Moncton, with campuses at Moncton, Shippegan and Edmunston. In Nova Scotia the only Acadian institution of higher learning is still Université Sainte-Anne at Church Point which is supported by the province and has a lay board of governors.

In the political arena

The Acadians did not enter the political arena before 1830, when Colonel Anselme Doucet submitted his candidacy as representative for the County of Annapolis, which at that time included the district of Clare, but he was not elected.

The first Acadians elected to the Assembly in the Maritimes were Simon d'Entremont and Frederic Robichaud in 1836. The first Acadian elected in New Brunswick was P.A. Landry, in 1846, and in Prince Edward Island the first Acadian elected to the legislature was Stanislaus Poirier in 1854.

From 1836 to the present time there has always been at least one Acadian member in the Legislative Assembly of the province of Nova Scotia, and as many as four. However, as in only two ridings do they form a majority, they seldom will get representation in proportion to their population. At the present time there are only three Acadians in the Assembly, the members for Clare Argyle and Yarmouth ridings.Two are cabinet members.

In Nova Scotia the Acadians have had at least one member in the cabinet most of the time since the beginning of this century.

In New Brunswick the Acadians were a long time getting their rightful representation in the Assembly, as the counties in which Acadians formed a majority had fewer members in relation to their population than the other counties. For example the county of Charlotte, in the English section of the province, with a population of 20,000 had four members, while Gloucester, an Acadian county, with a population of 17,000 had only one member. However the situation changed during the premiership of Hon. Louis Robichaud, and now that all the counties have representation in proportion to their population, the Acadians have their rightful share of members in the Assembly and in the Cabinet. Two Acadians, Hon. Pierre Veniot and Hon. Louis Robichaud, have been premiers, and two, Hon. Hédard Robichaud and Hon. Gilbert Finn, have been Lieutenant-Governors.

In Prince Edward Island the Acadians are a minority in all three counties, and are far from being able to elect members to the Assembly in proportion to their numbers. However, this province has had one Acadian premier, Hon. Aubin Arsenault, and two Acadian Lieutenant-Governors, Hon. Auguste Bernard and Hon. Aubin Doiron.

The Acadians of New Brunswick have been represented in the House of Commons since Confederation, and in the Senate since 1885. Prince Edward Island elected its only Acadian member of the House of Commons in 1873, Stanislaus Poirier, and its only senator, J.O. Arsenault, was appointed in 1895 and died the following year. Prince Edward Island Acadians have not had a representative in the federal government in this century.

Nova Scotia had its first Acadian senator in 1907, in the person of Hon. Ambroise H. Comeau, but the Acadians of this province did not elect one of theirs to the House of Commons before 1935, in the person of Hon. Vincent Pottier. Since 1907 the Acadians of Nova Scotia have always been represented in the Senate, but not always in the House of Commons.

At the present time the Acadians of New Brunswick and Nova Scotia have their rightful representation in the House of Commons and in the Senate, and enjoy considerable political clout in these two provinces. The Acadians of Prince Edward Island, having no representation in either the House of Commons or the Senate, and few members in their provincial legislature have found it difficult to get the attention they deserve for their just demands.

Acadian culture today

The Acadian cultural activities which had been dormant for more than a century after the Expulsion, revived in the 1880's. At the conventions of 1881 and 1884, at Memramcook and Miscouche, the Acadians of the Maritimes chose the Feast of the Assumption as their patron feast, the tricolor flag with the Star of the Sea as the Acadian banner and the Ave Maris Stella as their rallying anthem.

Following these conventions there was a real flowering of patriotic songs such as: *Evangéline, Le Pêcheur Acadien, Partons la mer est belle, l'Acadien Errant,* and many others. And writers expressed in prose and verse the sad and at the same time heroic story of the people.

Today the Acadian culture is manifested in the revival of Acadian songs and music by such talented composers and performers as Edith Butler, Donat LaCroix, Angele Arsenault, the groups Beausoleil-Broussard, 1755, Panou and many others. There is a lively and increasing interest in all the Acadian communities of the regional Acadian festivals which began in 1955 to mark the 200th anniversary of the expulsion.

Cultural associations such as the Société Nationale des Acadiens, L'Association des Acadiens du Nouveau-Brunswick, La Société Saint-Thomas d'Aquin in Prince Edward Island, La Société Saint-Pierre in Cape Breton, La Fédération Acadienne de la Nouvelle-Écosse, and the historical societies in every Acadian region keep the interest alive in the culture, and traditions, and history of this ethnic group.

Painting and sculpture and crafts are flourishing as galleries open in the Acadian regions, where artists and artisans may display and sell their works. Some of these artists have attained an international reputation such as Claude Roussel, Claude Picard, Nelson Surette, Leo B. LeBlanc, Elizabeth LeFort to name but a few who are making a name for themselves in the arts.

A strong Acadian literature has developed in the last thirty years. Acadians have now ventured into all literary fields, poetry, novels, short stories, history, drama and screen writing, and many have won national and international acclaim, notably Antonine Maillet, who won the Prix Goncourt, the most prestigious literary award in all French literature, the first woman and the first person outside France to win it.

While the rate of assimilation in some Acadian regions causes some concern, by and large Acadians express confidence in the survival and strengthening of their culture, by the motto which they adopted in 1980 to celebrate the 375th anniversary of the founding of Port Royal:

On est venus, c'est pour rester.
(We have come to stay)

Printed in Yarmouth
1992